D0119097

Discovering
Christopher Columbus

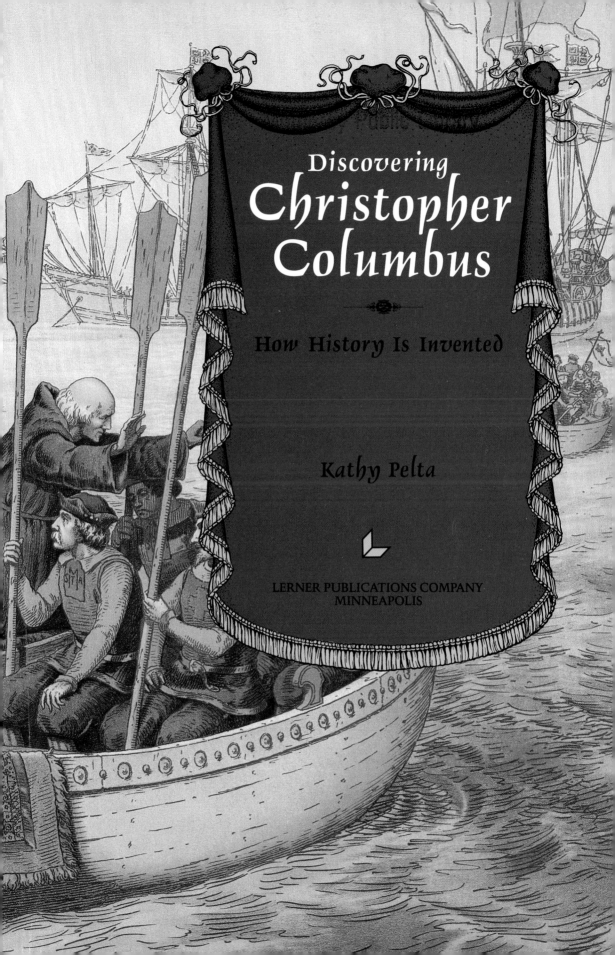

Discovering
Christopher
Columbus

How History Is Invented

Kathy Pelta

LERNER PUBLICATIONS COMPANY
MINNEAPOLIS

For my son Brian, who loves
history as much as I do

The author wishes to thank John Parker, curator of the
James Ford Bell Library of the University of Minnesota,
for his assistance in the preparation of this book. She is
also grateful for the help of local reference librarians.

Library of Congress Cataloging-in-Publication Data

Pelta, Kathy.
Discovering Christopher Columbus: how history is invented/
Kathy Pelta.
p.   cm.
Includes bibliographical references and index.
Summary: A biography of Christopher Columbus with emphasis on how
historians have worked and are still working to find out the truth
about his life and discoveries.
ISBN 0-8225-4899-2
1. Columbus, Christopher—Juvenile literature. 2. Explorers—
America—Biography—History and criticism—Juvenile literature.
3. Explorers—Spain—Biography—History and criticism—Juvenile
literature. 4. America—Discovery and exploration—Spanish—
Historiography—Juvenile literature. [1. Columbus, Christopher.
2. Explorers. 3. America—Discovery and exploration—Spanish—
Historiography.] I. Title.
E111.P414   1991
970.01′5—dc20
[B]   90-24165
[92]   CIP
                                                          AC

Manufactured in the United States of America

1 2 3 4 5 6 7 8 9 00 99 98 97 96 95 94 93 92 91

_C · 1_

CONTENTS

This statue of Columbus stands in Genoa, Italy, which is believed to be his home town.

INTRODUCTION

In Fourteen hundred and ninety-two,
Columbus sailed the ocean blue

HAT SHORT RHYME HELPS PEOPLE REMEMBER THE year Christopher Columbus first came to America. We know the date is correct: we have evidence to prove it—from eyewitness accounts to official Spanish government records.

But what about other details of Columbus's life? How can historians be sure of his birth date, or where he grew up, or who his parents were? Some people said he was a pirate. Was that true? Or, as some other early writers believed, was he born of nobility—the grandson of a duke, or even a prince? How can we find out what Columbus looked like, or what color his hair was? Did he have brothers and sisters? And what about the Native American people— the people Columbus called "Indians," who greeted him when he arrived in the so-called New World? Do we know how they felt when a boatload of strangers suddenly appeared, uninvited, on their shores?

The job of the historian is to learn about events and about people of the past—what they thought and said and did. This book tells how historians who wrote about Columbus went about their jobs.

Piecing together the Columbus story has not been easy. Five hundred years ago, when Columbus lived, there were few written records. Over time, the records that did exist were often lost or destroyed. To complicate matters even more, Columbus was in many ways a man of mystery. He did not tell people much about his family or his childhood. (Or if he did, his contemporaries didn't write it down in any document that anyone has so far discovered.) To find out the details of his life, historians had to become detectives. Hunting for clues, they sifted through old letters, wills, court records, letters, royal proclamations, and books written by people who lived at the time of Columbus and who knew him.

In their search for details about Columbus, historians ran into all sorts of problems: big problems, such as trying to separate the truth about the man from legend; and smaller ones, like the confusion over Columbus's name. In earlier days, standards of spelling changed from time to time and were not rigid. People were casual about how they spelled both proper names and ordinary words. Columbus was no exception. Besides this, during his lifetime he used several different names. The name Columbus used on a document depended on when and where the document was written.

This man whom English-speaking people call Christopher Columbus began life with the Italian name of Cristoforo Colombo. In Italy today that is still what people call him. Later he went to Portugal, where people knew him as Cristovão Colon or Colom, or sometimes Cristoforo Colomo. In Spain, he became Cristóval (or Cristóbal) Colón. On some official papers, he was called Christophorus Columbus—his name in Latin. That was because the notaries who recorded early legal documents wrote in Latin. So did learned authors. Since the first book about Columbus published in England was in Latin, people in England first knew him as Christophorus Columbus. Later they shortened his first name so he became Christopher Columbus, the name they still call him today. That is what we will call him in this book.

Piecing together the Columbus story has taken historians a long time—and they are not through yet. Each time they uncover some new fact—or each time a "fact" turns out *not* to be true—the story changes. And, once again, the historians need to update what was written about him.

As the Columbus story has changed through the years, so have people's feelings about him. In past centuries, many saw Columbus as a bigger-than-life superhero. Today few people are willing to accept a "superman" Christopher Columbus who can do no wrong. They recognize that, along with being brave and daring, he was disagreeable at times and not always truthful. We now know that Columbus also dealt in slavery, an accepted practice in his day. When he couldn't find enough gold in America to ship back to Spain, he captured hundreds of Arawak Indians and sent them back instead, to be sold in slave markets in Seville.

Earlier writers tended to gloss over this darker side of Columbus. And they all but ignored the feelings of the people who were so shamefully mistreated by Columbus and the Spanish settlers and soldiers who invaded their lands. Modern historians try to tell the whole story—including the point of view of the Indians.

Besides dealing with important social and moral questions, historians continue trying to solve riddles about Columbus the man. For example, where did Columbus first land? In his own writings, Columbus was vague about the landfall island. He gave very little description and no longitude. After five centuries, historians still cannot agree on which island in the West Indies it might have been. The true answer may never be known.

Then there is the confusion over Columbus's bones. Where *are* they? The mystery began a few years after Columbus's death, when the casket with his remains was moved from its original resting place. The casket was moved three more times after that—including trips across the Atlantic to the New World and back to Spain again. Some scholars believe that the bones of Columbus may now be in at least seven different places!

And what about Columbus's puzzling signature? What does it mean? To this day, no one is sure. Solving that and all of the other Columbus puzzles will be up to future historians.

Columbus may have grown up in this house, which stands in an old section of Genoa.

ONE

CHRISTOPHER COLUMBUS

I F YOU WERE A HISTORIAN TODAY, AND YOU WANTED to learn about Columbus, where would you go first? To the library, of course!

Not so, if you had lived back in the 1500s. Then, there were no public libraries. But now, libraries—with their many books and magazines and newspapers—are where all historians begin their research. And so should you.

If the library in your town or school is small, it does not matter. Features such as interlibrary loans allow you to borrow information from libraries in other places. And even the smallest library is sure to have one important reference source: an encyclopedia. To start learning about Columbus all you have to do is find the volume of "C's." Then look up *Columbus, Christopher.*

The entry in an encyclopedia will give you a good overview of Columbus's life. This overview has details that historians have learned about Columbus so far.

Historians began to retell the story of Christopher Columbus back in the 1500s, soon after he died. Over the centuries, the "true story" has changed many times. What schoolchildren knew about Columbus in the 1500s and 1600s is not the same as what you can read about him today. For historians keep finding out new things.

In fact, to really understand Columbus's life and deeds, historians must go back in history to events that happened many years before Columbus was born. In 1417, Henry the Navigator, a prince of Portugal, eagerly began to push for exploration. He funded voyage after voyage along the coast of Africa. He had a number of reasons for this passion: he wanted to find out about lands no European had seen before; he hoped to establish regular trade with African peoples; and, because he was a good Christian, he also wanted to introduce Christianity to new lands and to learn more about any enemies of the Christians. By the time Columbus was born, Henry the Navigator's explorers had added hundreds of miles of African coastline to the maps of European sailors.

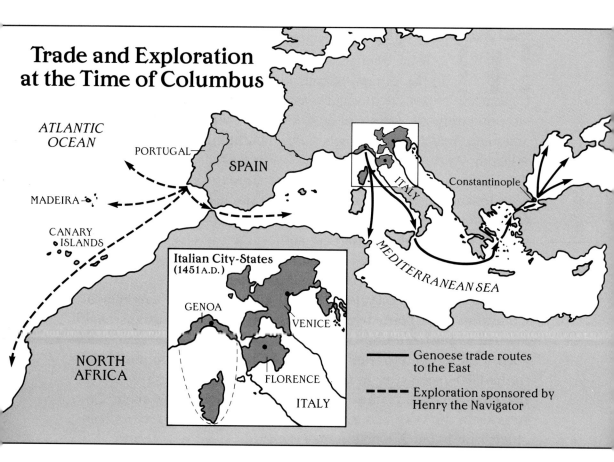

Trade and Exploration at the Time of Columbus

ATLANTIC OCEAN

PORTUGAL

SPAIN

MADEIRA

CANARY ISLANDS

ITALY

Constantinople

MEDITERRANEAN SEA

Italian City-States (1451 A.D.)

GENOA

VENICE

FLORENCE

ITALY

NORTH AFRICA

——————— Genoese trade routes to the East

- - - - - Exploration sponsored by Henry the Navigator

This engraving from 1880 is based on a painting of the young Christopher Columbus that was done long after his death.

The story of Columbus's early life that most people today accept as true begins in Genoa in the year 1451. It was a time before Italy was a country, when Genoa was an independent city-state. A city-state is a country made up of a city and some of the surrounding land. Besides Genoa, other well-known city-states in this area were Florence and Venice.

The Republic of Genoa was known in 1451 as a trading center for goods from the Far East. Genoese traders brought in Oriental spices and fabrics and other luxuries for sale all over Europe. The trip west to Europe from the Orient was long, dangerous, and difficult, whether the goods traveled by ships or across deserts and mountains in caravans. This made the goods very expensive, but cinnamon and silk were so popular that Genoa became rich shipping these goods into Europe.

Sometime between August and the end of October of 1451, a son was born to the weaver Domenico Colombo and his wife Susanna in Genoa. They named the baby Cristoforo (the Italian name for Christopher). Before long, the Colombos had three more sons and a daughter.

Christopher and his brothers and sister probably did not go to school. In those days only children of rich families could afford schooling, and Domenico Colombo and his wife had very little money. If Christopher had any formal training at all, it may have been at a guild school, where the children of craftsmen could learn some arithmetic, a few Latin phrases, and how to write their names. Most of the time, Christopher no doubt worked in his father's weaving shop. He would have carded wool, combing out the burrs and muddy tangles so his mother could spin it into yarn for the weaver's loom. But whenever he finished work early, it is likely that the red-haired boy raced to the docks. For his real love was sailing. As he watched ships come and go, as he listened to sailors spin yarns of a different sort, he could dream of the day he would be a seaman. Then he could lead his own life of high adventure!

And exciting things were happening at sea. Exploration had gotten a boost from world events. When Columbus was a baby, the Turks had conquered Constantinople and gained control of all the known trade routes to the East. The Muslim Turks refused to let Christian traders cross their lands or their seas. The price of the silks and spices that the Europeans so loved had risen sharply.

Something must be done! Perhaps when he watched ships unloading European olives or wool at Genoese docks, Columbus dreamed of ways to fill them with more exotic cargoes of nutmeg or silk from the Orient.

Before he was 20, Columbus did go to sea. For about five years he worked on cargo ships in the Mediterranean. Sailing from port to port, he watched closely and learned sailors' skills: how to "hand, reef and steer" a sailing vessel, how to set and weigh (raise) an anchor, and how to judge distances by eye. Then Columbus signed on as a seaman on a trading vessel bound for northern Europe. For the first time, he ventured onto the Atlantic Ocean. But as the trade ship was passing Portugal's coast, an enemy ship sank it. Columbus jumped into the water. He grabbed a floating oar for a life preserver and kicked his way six miles (nine and a half kilometers) to shore.

He landed at the small town of Lagos, where he stayed until he was well enough to move on. Then he went to live in Lisbon, Portugal's main seaport. His host there may have been his younger brother Bartholomew, who was probably already in the chart- and mapmaking business. Sailors needed to have new charts and their old charts updated as explorers made new discoveries in the Atlantic Ocean and along the African coastline.

Again Columbus took up the seafaring life—this time on Portuguese ships. He sailed into the North Atlantic to Bristol, England. He later claimed he went as far north as Iceland, a small island on the Arctic Circle. Between voyages, he helped his brother run the chart shop in Lisbon.

Christopher Columbus taught himself to read and write the

language that the educated people of Lisbon used. It was not Portuguese, but a form of Spanish called Castilian. Around 1480 Columbus married Felipa Perestrello e Moniz, daughter of a Portuguese nobleman, and they went to live on the island of Porto Santo off the west coast of Africa. Here he began to work on a plan to sail west to the Orient, or "the Indies" as it was then called.

His problem would be finding a rich patron to cover the cost of the very risky voyage. The difficulty was not to convince a patron that the world was round, nor to assure people that the expedition would not "sail off the edge." Almost all educated people knew this already. The problem Columbus faced was to persuade someone with funds that the world was the size Columbus thought it was. The map he used in his planning showed the Orient to be 3,000 miles (4,830 km) from Europe. And that was what Columbus believed.

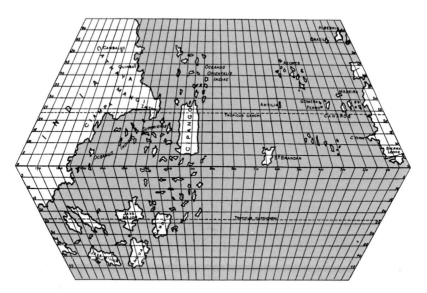

Columbus thought the world was as it appears on this map from 1474. Europe is at the far right; Hibernia, at the top, is Scotland. In the center left, the large island, Cipango, is Japan. The ocean between Europe and Asia, thought to be the only ocean in the world, was called "the Ocean Sea."

Columbus naturally went to the very top with his plan. Not only did kings and queens have plenty of money for an expedition, but they controlled the trade routes and could grant Columbus exclusive rights to trading areas. When Columbus tried to sell his plan to Portugal's King John, however, the king's royal experts advised against it. They knew the size of the world better than some unknown seaman from Genoa did! And they were right. The true distance to Asia west from Europe was more like 10,000 miles (16,000 km).

Columbus's wife died, then his money began to run out, so he saw no reason to stay in Portugal. Since Portugal did not want his plan, he would offer it to Spain.

With his five-year-old son, Diego, Columbus sailed to the Spanish port of Palos in 1485. Monks at a nearby monastery agreed to care for little Diego while Columbus went to see the Spanish sovereigns, Isabella and Ferdinand. Unfortunately, the sovereigns had

Columbus explains his theory to the monks at La Rábida, the monastery where he left Diego (right). The monks later introduced him to a powerful man who helped him gain the attention of the sovereigns.

This is a portrait of Columbus with his sons Diego and Ferdinand.
The woman in the portrait is sometimes identified as Beatriz
Enríquez de Harana.

no time to talk to Columbus — or Cristóbal Colón, as he was known in Spain. The very Christian Queen Isabella and her husband were busy trying to drive the Muslim Moors from Spanish soil.

The war went on and Columbus waited. After a year, he finally saw the queen, and in May 1486 he presented his case. She appointed a special commission of advisers to consider Columbus's request. The commission heard Columbus in Salamanca in 1486 but could not decide how to advise the queen. A year passed with no report. Little is known about what he did during those years he waited for the queen and king to decide about his great enterprise. But we do know he met a Spanish woman named Beatriz Enríquez de Harana. They had a son, Ferdinand, born in 1488. By then, Columbus decided the Spanish sovereigns had dawdled long enough.

Maybe he should try Portugal again. So he wrote to King John, who invited him back to Portugal.

The very month Columbus arrived back in Lisbon, an explorer named Bartolomeu Dias sailed into the harbor. Dias told of finding a passage around the southern tip of Africa to the Indian Ocean. If his crew had not insisted they return to Lisbon, Dias might have gone clear to India. The king of Portugal was delighted.

The passage Dias had found was called the Cape of Good Hope. For Columbus, alas, it meant "no more hope." For why would Portugal need his plan for sailing west to the Indies? Now it had a sea route east to the Indies. Discouraged, Columbus went back to Spain.

When he returned to Spain, the commission was still not ready to report to the sovereign on his project. It was more than a year before they were ready—and then they advised against it. The queen did give Columbus hope, however. She told him that when the war was over, he could ask again.

After another year, and another commission's report, finally the queen said yes. She even said they would give him three ships, and if his enterprise was a success he would receive important titles. The sovereigns promised that much of the "gold, silver, pearls, gems, spices and other merchandise" taken from lands he discovered would be his.

Columbus went to Palos harbor on Spain's southwest coast. There he made ready for the journey. Martín Pinzón, who lived in Palos, was a big help in recruiting almost 100 crewmen for the voyage.

On August 3, 1492, Columbus's fleet of three small wooden vessels set sail from Palos. Martín Pinzón and his brother, Vicente, commanded the small, light, and speedy caravels *Niña* and *Pinta*. Columbus sailed on the larger and slower flagship, *Santa María*, which was a *nao*, or ship, not a caravel.

Nearly every day of the voyage, Columbus wrote in his journal, or log, about whatever he "might do and see and experience . . . from day to day."

One entry records how restless the crewmen grew, after several weeks at sea with no sight of land.

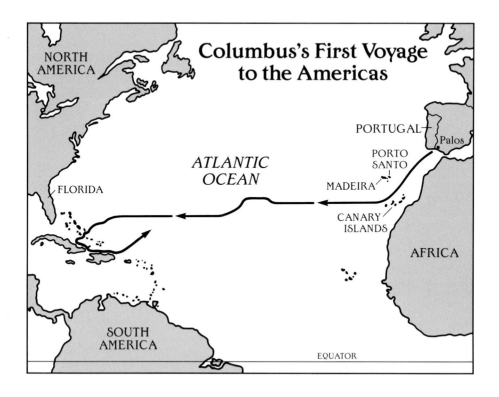

Columbus's First Voyage to the Americas

NORTH AMERICA

PORTUGAL

Palos

PORTO SANTO

ATLANTIC OCEAN

MADEIRA

FLORIDA

CANARY ISLANDS

AFRICA

SOUTH AMERICA

EQUATOR

"*Adelante*! Forward! Sail on!!" they were told.

When the men still did not sight land, they became even more restless and threatened mutiny. Columbus cheered them as best he could. He and Martín Pinzón conferred and finally decided to "carry on for some days."

Columbus promised a reward—money and a handsome new coat—to the first man to sight land. Then they started to see signs that land was close, such as floating branches and flocks of land birds. The grumbling about a mutiny ceased.

A few days later, on October 12, 1492, there were shouts of "*Tierra*! —Land!" The tiny fleet had reached an island in the Bahamas off the coast of present-day Florida. Columbus claimed the reward for being the first to sight land, saying he had seen a light in the west hours earlier. Columbus named the island San Salvador and went ashore to claim the island for Spain. Friendly people greeted him.

In this Italian engraving from the 1800s, Columbus gives thanks for reaching the Indies.

Columbus noted in his journal that the Arawak Indians "bear no arms [weapons]... they remained so much our friends that it was a marvel... they brought us parrots and cotton thread and many other things." Columbus called them Indians, for he believed he was in the Indies.

The fleet then sailed on to explore nearby islands, including one that reminded Columbus so much of Spain that he named it La Isla Española. Soon after, people began calling it Hispaniola. It was on the shore of Hispaniola that the *Santa María* ran aground on Christmas Eve. The Arawaks helped the crewmen recover supplies from the wrecked ship, and they used lumber from the ship to build a fort. Columbus named the fort La Navidad, the Spanish word for Christmas.

With only two ships able to return to Spain, some men had to stay at La Navidad. They didn't mind, however. By then gold had been found on a nearby island, and the men were eager to search for more.

On the return voyage, Columbus, aboard the *Niña*, became separated from Martín Pinzón, commanding the *Pinta*. The voyage back was difficult, and the *Niña* fought its way through storm after storm. During a violent squall, Columbus wrote a letter to Isabella and Ferdinand telling of his adventures. He sealed the letter in a wooden barrel, which he dropped into the sea. If he didn't survive the storm, at least the barrel might—and the sovereigns would know of his discovery.

As it turned out, neither cask nor contents were ever seen again. But the *Niña* did reach Palos harbor. On solid ground once more, Columbus sent another letter to the king and queen telling of the wonders he had seen.

A few hours after the *Niña* dropped anchor in the harbor, the *Pinta* also arrived at Palos. Earlier, Martín Pinzón had stopped at another Spanish port to send a message to the sovereigns, but they replied that they did not choose to receive Pinzón until Columbus had also returned. Martín Pinzón, who was ill, left his ship at Palos and went straight home. He took to his bed and died soon after.

Meanwhile, Columbus went to Seville and waited for the sovereigns in Barcelona to answer his letter. Even a famous explorer would not barge into the royal palace without an invitation. The letter from the sovereigns arrived at last. They addressed it to: "Don Cristóbal Colón, their Admiral of the Ocean Sea, Viceroy and Governor of the Islands that he hath discovered in the Indies." "Don" was a Spanish title of honor. "Admiral of the Ocean Sea" meant he "ruled" the Atlantic Ocean (except for parts Portugal controlled). And as "Viceroy and Governor of the Islands," he was in charge there, too!

The sovereigns invited Columbus to Barcelona, where they were holding court. It was 800 miles (over 1,000 km) from Seville, so, on foot and by horseback, Columbus made his way there during the spring of 1493. As he passed through the Spanish countryside, people gathered along the dusty roads to watch the colorful procession. They admired Columbus, splendid in his elegant uniform. They gawked at the hired servants carrying gold and spices, and at the six Indians wearing bright feathers and ornaments of fish bone and gold and carrying parrots in cages.

To the Spanish people that spring of 1493, Columbus was a hero—much like today's John Glenn, first United States astronaut to orbit in outer space, or like Charles Lindbergh, the first airplane pilot to fly solo across the Atlantic.

When Columbus reached the royal palace, he presented the queen with his journal. The queen and king then allowed him to sit in their presence. They gave him a grand reception and listened eagerly to all that he had to say. Others at court listened, too. The royal tutor, Peter Martyr, was full of questions. Soon after, Martyr wrote to friends on the Italian peninsula to spread the news of Columbus's triumphant return.

Things would not go this well for Christopher Columbus ever again!

Columbus shows the Spanish sovereigns his proof that he has found the Indies: people wearing feathers and strange clothes; exotic flowers; pipes for breathing in smoke of burning leaves; gold jewelry; strange pottery, tools, and weapons.

—◆ TWO ◆—

THE OTHER VOYAGES

1493-1506

EFORE COLUMBUS REACHED BARCELONA, THE sovereigns had already sent the letter he wrote to them to a printer. Within a year the four-page letter had been reprinted many times, and in several languages. It became a "best-seller."

Columbus had been vague about the exact route he had sailed. That was to keep explorers from other countries from going there to try to take over some of Spain's new lands. As proof that he had actually reached the Indies, Columbus gave details in the letter about how the natives had assured him that the Great Khan, China's ruler, was nearby.

Although Columbus did not mention the shipwreck of the *Santa María*, he did tell about the fort he had built at La Navidad and about the men he had left there with "artillery and provisions for more than a year."

In the letter, Columbus described the exotic trees and plants he had found and the "nightingales . . . and other little birds of a thousand kinds." He said there were "great and good streams, most of which bear gold." And he told of "people without number . . . well-built people of handsome stature, artless and so free with all they possess . . . and naked . . . as their mothers bore them."

When people read Columbus's published letter, the two features that fascinated them most were those naked Indians—and the gold! What delighted the very religious Queen Isabella were all the new souls Catholic priests could now convert to Christianity. Isabella and Ferdinand wanted Columbus to hurry back to the Indies to start a colony. This time, the sovereigns said, they would help him outfit a fleet of 17 ships. That way there would be space to transport workers, seeds to plant, and animals such as dogs, sheep, cattle, goats, geese, chickens, hogs, and horses.

For his second voyage, Columbus had no trouble getting crews. There were plenty of volunteers, including his younger brother Diego. The trip started off well. The fleet left Spain in the fall of 1493. Instead of heading straight for Hispaniola, they explored islands along the way. Columbus and the others admired the strange and beautiful trees and flowers and tasted their first pineapple.

But at Hispaniola, Columbus found trouble. The fort on the island was destroyed. All of the crewmen he had left there a few months before were gone. Columbus and his men found several bodies. Later an Indian reported what had happened. The Spaniards left at the fort had robbed the Arawaks and treated them so badly in other ways that the angered natives had killed them all.

Columbus ordered a new town built on another part of the island. He named it Isabela, after his queen. Leaving his brother Diego in charge of the new settlement, Columbus took a fleet of three ships to explore other islands. He planned to look for gold as well as to finally find the great and wealthy cities he was sure were nearby.

From Hispaniola, Columbus sailed along the southern coast of Cuba, where he found neither cities nor gold. Since Cuba's coastline was so long, Columbus decided it must be the mainland of Japan. He made his crew sign statements that they, too, believed this land was part of the continent of Asia, for never had anyone known an island that large. Columbus threatened that if any man ever "said the contrary" he would be fined 10,000 maravedis—the equivalent of several years' salary. Even worse, the seaman would

Left, pineapple was first seen by Europeans on Columbus's second voyage to the Indies. Illustration from Oviedo's history. Right, Columbus talks to a cacique, or chief, on the island of Cuba.

have his tongue cut out. If he were a boy, he would be given 100 lashes on his bare back!

Returning to Isabela on Hispaniola, Columbus was delighted to find that his brother Bartholomew had finally arrived. However, he also found the colony in chaos. His brother Diego had not managed the colony well. The colonists, in their frantic search for gold, had overworked and killed many Indians—yet found little gold. Columbus needed to send something back to the sovereigns, to "repay [them] for their great expenses." So he ordered hundreds of natives captured. In place of gold, he would send Indian slaves to the slave market in Seville.

Columbus put Bartholomew in charge of the colony. He ordered

A 16th-century map shows the settlement of Santo Domingo, located at the mouth of the Ozama River. The settlers built walls around the town to protect it from increasingly unfriendly Taino Indians.

Bartholomew to abandon Isabela, though, and to start yet another settlement, to be called Santo Domingo.

Then Columbus left Hispaniola and returned to Spain. He stayed for a time with his friend Andrés Bernáldez, a Catholic curate, or churchman. Columbus told Bernáldez about his adventures and left his journals and papers for Bernáldez to use for a history the curate was writing.

By this time, Columbus was not a hero to the Spanish people as he had been before. What he had done no longer seemed so amazing. Now other explorers were making discoveries just as exciting. In 1497 the Portuguese explorer Vasco da Gama had rounded the Cape of Good Hope and sailed clear to India.

Vasco da Gama's accomplishment made some people doubt that Columbus had actually reached the Indies. Maybe what he had found was not the Indies after all. Columbus still insisted it was. And he would prove it as soon as he found the mainland of China or Japan. He asked the sovereigns to send him back there a third time to look for it. And they did, in 1498.

On this third voyage, Columbus discovered more islands in the Caribbean. But the only mainland he found was South America.

Thinking it must be the Garden of Eden, he called it an "Other World."

A few days later, Columbus landed at Santo Domingo, the colony on Hispaniola. There he found the angry colonists in revolt. Life had not been as easy as they had expected. They were tired of the native food. They hated the living conditions. They were not finding much gold. And they were tired of having Columbus in charge.

The unrest at Santo Domingo became so violent that a group of the Spanish joined with unhappy Tainos in rebellion against the rule of the Columbus brothers. In an attempt to restore order, the brothers had some of these rebels hanged.

Christopher Columbus is put in chains at the order of the sovereigns' envoy, to be sent back to Spain. One story goes that the envoy asked for volunteers to put the chains on Columbus, and Columbus's cook offered to do the deed.

Those who had gone back to Spain had spread the word that the Columbus brothers were terrible governors and that there was trouble in the colony. By then, Isabella and Ferdinand were losing patience with Columbus. For seven years he had promised them riches—yet so far all he had brought them were expenses. And now there was this trouble in the colony.

The sovereigns sent an envoy, their personal representative, to settle the problem. He settled it by arresting Columbus and shipping him home in chains. Queen Isabella ordered the chains taken off soon after Columbus reached Spain, though after that she and Ferdinand were never as friendly with Columbus. When he asked them to return him to Hispaniola as governor once more, they did not reply.

Others turned against Columbus. In Spain he had more enemies

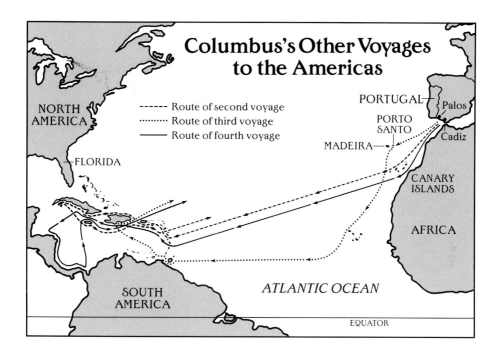

than friends. People teased his two sons, Diego and Ferdinand, calling them "sons of the Admiral of the Mosquitoes." In Santo Domingo, Hispaniola, it was no better. Unhappy colonists began to spread the rumor that Columbus was not the true discoverer of the Indies. The real discoverer, people said, was a ship's pilot—the special assistant on a ship who helps the captain decide the best course to follow. This pilot, the rumormongers said, had found an island far out in the Ocean Sea. The pilot's ship had been wrecked. All of the others aboard had died. But the pilot had managed to make it back to Portugal, where he had revealed his secret to Columbus—and then died.

If Columbus knew about this rumor, he did not admit it. And he did not let it bother him. Already he was planning a fourth voyage to the Indies. He asked the queen and king to approve it. This time, he assured them, he would find a way to sail clear to the Indian Ocean and the mainland of China or Japan.

The sovereigns agreed. They said Columbus was to discover

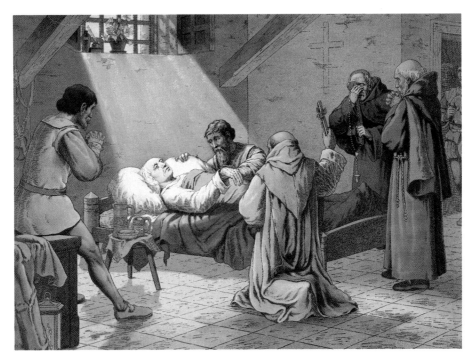

Columbus died soon after his fourth voyage to the Americas, and only 18 months after the death of Queen Isabella. He was buried in Valladolid, Spain, the town where he died.

islands and continents "in the Indies in the part that belongs to us"—but he was not to stop at Hispaniola.

In 1502 Christopher Columbus sailed west once more, this time with a fleet of four aging caravels. On this trip he took his younger son, 12-year-old Ferdinand. In vain Columbus searched for a waterway to the Indian Ocean. Then, as his fleet sailed along the Jamaican coast, the old ships began to leak. When the crews could no longer keep them afloat, they ran the ships ashore. Ferdinand described how the men brought the ships in as far as they could, "grounding them close together board and board, and shoring them up on both sides so they could not budge."

Here Columbus and his crew were marooned. Although several men quickly set off on the long and hazardous canoe trip to

Hispaniola to ask for help, it was a year before they were rescued.

Columbus arrived home in Spain in November 1504. By now, he was 53 and not well. He'd had a lifetime of adventure, but his days of travel were over. Even so, once he returned to Spain, the ailing and crotchety old admiral still stubbornly swore "by San Fernando" that those new lands he had discovered *were* the Indies!

Columbus spent the last years of his life trying to get the sovereigns to restore his "rights and privileges." Even though he was still called admiral and had a good income from the gold mines in the New World, Columbus wanted more. He wanted to be called viceroy, as the sovereigns had promised. And he wanted the power and income that went with the title.

The sovereigns ignored his pleas. This time even Isabella, always sympathetic before, would not listen to Columbus. She died soon after his return to Spain. After that, it was even worse for him, because the king would have nothing more to do with Columbus.

Christopher Columbus died on May 20, 1506, with only family and a few friends at his side. No royal envoys came to pay their respects. In the listing of important events of the day, there was no mention of his funeral and burial at a church in Valladolid, Spain.

Now that his life was over, it was up to historians to begin sifting through the evidence, looking for clues—so that they could tell the Columbus story to the world.

——— ❧ THREE ❧ ———

THROUGH
THE COURTS

1506-1599

I F YOU WERE A HISTORIAN IN THE EARLY 1500s AND wanted to learn about Christopher Columbus, you would have a hard time collecting information. When he died, there were no newspapers or television stations to recap his life and adventures. The New World he had discovered wasn't even named after him. Instead, it was named for Amerigo Vespucci, who sailed to Venezuela in 1499 and later reported these were unknown lands. Columbus, by insisting that Other World he had found was part of the well-known Indies, had missed his chance to have two continents named after him. In 1507, the name "America" appeared on these new lands on a world map.

Few people were even aware when, three years after Columbus's death, his family had his remains moved from Valladolid to a monastery near Seville. And it was seven more years before the first public mention of his death was made—in a history book.

In your search for information, you couldn't ask the government for help. It did not allow ordinary people to look at records in the royal archives. Also, Columbus was so unpopular with the royal government that in 1513 the Crown did an extraordinary thing. It went to the law courts to try to prove that Martín Pinzón—and not Columbus—was the one who made the enterprise to the Indies a success.

As an early historian, you could learn some things about Columbus's voyages from three letters that were published during his lifetime: the one Columbus wrote to the sovereigns after the first voyage ended in 1493; one he sent to them in 1503 by way of canoe to Hispaniola while he was marooned on Jamaica during his fourth voyage; and a letter a shipmate on the second voyage wrote to a friend back home. That letter was translated into Latin and printed in 1494.

To find out anything more about Columbus, you would have to talk with people who knew him—if you could find any.

Fortunately, five men who knew him, or knew people who knew him, wrote books about Columbus. No one man had all of the facts, but each had enough to say to make his book worthwhile.

A map of Hispaniola from the first "decade," or volume, of Peter Martyr's history. It shows the early settlements on the island, La Navidad and Isabela ("Nativita" and "Isabella Vecchia," both on the north coast), as well as Santo Domingo ("S. Dominico" on the south coast).

One man was an eyewitness. Another lived in the colony Columbus founded. Several were friends.

Peter Martyr was the first of these men to write about Columbus's discovery of the New World. He was the royal tutor who asked Columbus all those questions when the two met at the palace in Barcelona in 1493. Since Peter Martyr was given a firsthand account of the voyages, he could write as if "under the direction of Columbus himself" (as another historian put it). Peter Martyr began writing his history in 1494. The first volume, or decade, of his history appeared in 1511. In the second decade, published in 1516, the death of Columbus was mentioned in print for the first time. Many Europeans first learned about Columbus from Peter Martyr's writings. Like all good scholars of his day, Peter Martyr wrote in Latin. So the Latin "Christophorus Columbus" became Christopher Columbus when his history was translated into English in 1555.

Another early historian who wrote about Columbus was a colonist and official "historian of the Indies." Gonzalo Fernández de Oviedo sailed to the West Indies from Spain in 1512 and lived there most of his life. As a boy of 15, Oviedo had seen Columbus in 1493 in Barcelona, but they never met. Instead, this historian learned about Columbus and the voyages from talking to Columbus's shipmates. Oviedo was also an artist, and, to accompany the descriptions of animals and plants of the islands, he made sketches. Like many of his fellow colonists, he believed that some earlier discoverer might

Indians panning for gold as illustrated for Oviedo's history

have found the Indies before Columbus went there—which meant Christopher Columbus was not the true discoverer. (Although Oviedo believed the Indies had belonged to Spain before Columbus's time, he did not believe the rumor about the dying boat pilot who gave Columbus a secret map. He called that rumor false.)

The third of the early historians to write about Columbus was Bartolomé de Las Casas. He first saw Columbus in the spring of 1493 when Las Casas was 19. He watched the explorer's triumphant entrance into Seville. Las Casas remembered "beautiful green parrots, guaycas or masks made of precious stone and fish bone... sizeable samples of very fine gold and many other things never before seen in Spain."

In the fall of 1493, Las Casas's father and uncle sailed on Columbus's second voyage to the Indies. They became colonists, and Las Casas joined them there a few years later. He intended to be a planter. Instead, in 1510 he became the first Catholic priest to be ordained in the New World. Along with his life's work of helping the Indians, he wrote a history. It took him many years. He finally finished

These "Cruelties us'd by Spaniards on the Indians" are from the English translation of Las Casas's book. The cruelties include hanging them over a fire, chopping off hands, and more.

the manuscript in 1563, when he was almost 90, but it was not published until 1825. The priest used material from Peter Martyr's history. He also talked with Columbus's two sons, Ferdinand and Diego, and studied Columbus's papers and journals.

The fourth of these early historians was Andrés Bernáldez, the curate Columbus stayed with after his second voyage. The curate was fascinated by Columbus's stories and retold them in his history. He described the "properties" Columbus had brought back for the sovereigns—"two Indians, much ornate gold jewelry, and cages of screeching, brightly colored parrots." The curate also used material from the papers Columbus had left with him between voyages. The curate's history, like the one Las Casas wrote, was not published until the 1800s.

The fifth early historian—the eyewitness—was Ferdinand, Columbus's son. When Ferdinand was only 12, he went on the fourth voyage. He was 17 when Columbus died. Ferdinand kept all of his father's papers and journals, and he later used them to write a biography of Columbus. Ferdinand began writing his book late in his life, but it is not known exactly when. The *Historie*, as it was later called, was not published until 1571, long after Ferdinand had died.

Ferdinand said that one reason he wrote his father's history was to counter the tall tales others had told about Columbus. Ferdinand was offended by an Italian bishop who suggested Christopher Columbus was an "artisan" of "humble origin." Not so! protested Ferdinand. He said his father, "the Admiral," was "a learned man of great experience [who] did not waste his time in manual or mechanical labor." He explained that Columbus's parents had been "persons of worth made poor by wars in the area." In the biography, Ferdinand hinted—but did not actually say—that Columbus probably descended from royalty.

In this book Ferdinand also scolded the historian Oviedo for claiming that Spain owned the Indies before Columbus made his first voyage. That was "a great lie," declared Ferdinand.

These five early historians wrote very different things about Columbus. They did not even agree on what Columbus looked like.

One writer recalled Columbus's eyes were bright blue; another said they were gray, while a third said Columbus had "eyes lively." Ferdinand remembered only that his father's eyes were "light." He went on to describe his father's nose as "aquiline," that is, curved or hooked, and he said Columbus was "well-built, of more than average height." Another historian called him "tall."

All of the early historians did agree that Columbus had a ruddy complexion (with freckles, one of them noted). Most agreed that his hair was red when he was a young man and turned white by the time he was 30. One writer claimed this was due to Columbus's "anxiety." Another said it was because of "his labors."

Columbus's son Ferdinand also told what his father said when he was angry. Columbus was "an enemy of swearing," wrote Ferdinand, and he never heard his father utter any oath besides "By San Fernando" or "May God take you."

The five early historians knew very little about Columbus's youth. Ferdinand explained that Columbus "chose to leave in obscurity all that related to his birthplace." But to Ferdinand it did not matter where the great man came from. What mattered, said Ferdinand, was "the remarkable thing he did."

On some details about Columbus's early life, Ferdinand's facts were shaky. For example, he said that his father had gone to the University of Pavia as a young man. Later historians sifted through new evidence and concluded that Columbus was probably illiterate when he left home. They think he taught himself to read and write after he went to live in Portugal when he was in his late 20s.

While these early historians were writing about Columbus, the Crown went on holding hearings in the law court. At these legal hearings, called *pleitos* (or pleadings), the Crown brought in crewmen and others who knew Columbus to testify that his role in the discovery of the New World was less important than that of Martín Pinzón.

Witnesses for the Crown said that without the help of Martín Pinzón, Columbus would never have found a crew for that first voyage. Pinzón was from Palos, and people trusted him, whereas Columbus was Genoese—an outsider.

Left, Vicente Yáñez Pinzón, who commanded the Niña *on the first voyage, and right, Martín Alonso Pinzón, who commanded the* Pinta. *Their portraits hang in the naval museum in Madrid.*

One witness for the Crown, a seaman who had gone on that first voyage, said that when the men were afraid and they wanted to turn back, he heard Martín Pinzón tell Columbus, "*Adelante, adelante,* I don't hold with turning back without sighting land."

Then Columbus's older son, Diego, brought in people to testify in Columbus's favor. Ferdinand Columbus was the keeper of his father's papers, so he could provide these witnesses with Christopher Columbus's word on what really happened.

All of this court testimony had one important benefit for later historians. It gave them useful information of all kinds. For example, one witness who testified during the hearings had been in Palos when Columbus came to the monastery from Lisbon in 1485. He told how Columbus "journeyed on foot to La Rábida" with his son Diego, and "asked at the gate for bread and water to drink for the small child...." It is a story that has since been retold many times in history books and biographies of Columbus.

Another witness at the hearings had been on Columbus's second voyage. He described the provisions, giving present-day historians a better idea about what kinds of supplies were aboard Columbus's ships.

As the court battle between the Columbus family and the Crown continued, Diego also sued the Crown to get back the title of viceroy that the king had taken away from his father. Diego argued that as Columbus's son and legal heir he should receive the title.

And what difference did it make who won? To Diego Columbus, winning meant he would get the revenues from all of the viceroy's fields and gold mines in the New World. That was just what the Crown did not want. If it won, it could keep all those revenues.

The *pleitos* dragged on for years. After Diego died, in 1526, his son Luis (Columbus's grandson) took up the fight. It lasted for another 10 years. In the end, Luis Columbus lost. In 1536 he agreed to settle for only a small amount of land and the less important title of duke of Veragua. Useful as they were to historians, the *pleitos* did not restore Columbus's original titles or resolve who shouted "*Adelante!* Sail on!"

Soon after the hearings ended, María, the widow of Diego Columbus, requested permission from the government to carry out the last request of her husband that he be buried in Hispaniola. She also asked permission to take the remains of her father-in-law, Christopher Columbus, to the colony. After much delay and argument, the government gave the widow permission. The remains of both Diego and Christopher Columbus were removed from their burial places in Spain. They were repacked in small lead caskets and taken by ship to Hispaniola. There they were buried before the high altar of the Santo Domingo cathedral.

While Luis Columbus, Columbus's grandson, was still a minor, his mother, María, was in control of all of the family papers. These included Columbus's charts, letters, legal records, and the manuscript of Ferdinand Columbus's biography of his father. Also in the collection was the only known copy of Columbus's journal (log) of the first voyage; the original of the log was not seen again after he gave it to Queen Isabella in 1493.

A statue of Christopher Columbus now stands outside the cathedral in Santo Domingo where Christopher, his son Diego, and his grandson Luis were buried.

After María died, Luis Columbus eventually acquired all of the family papers. This was unfortunate. For Luis was more concerned with drinking and gambling than with preserving these valuable documents. Their only value to him, apparently, was how much money they would bring if he sold them.

The copy of Columbus's journal, or log, known today as the Barcelona copy, has been lost. It was probably sold by Luis Columbus to the highest bidder, though no one knows for sure. Historians do know that Luis sold the manuscript of Ferdinand's biography of Columbus to a physician in Genoa. The physician had it printed in Venice, in Italian, in 1571.

By the end of the 1500s, people in Spain had grown more sympathetic to Columbus. In a play about Columbus's discovery by the popular Spanish playwright Lope de Vega, the character of Martín Pinzón was portrayed as the villain—the one who plotted with crewmen to mutiny against Columbus.

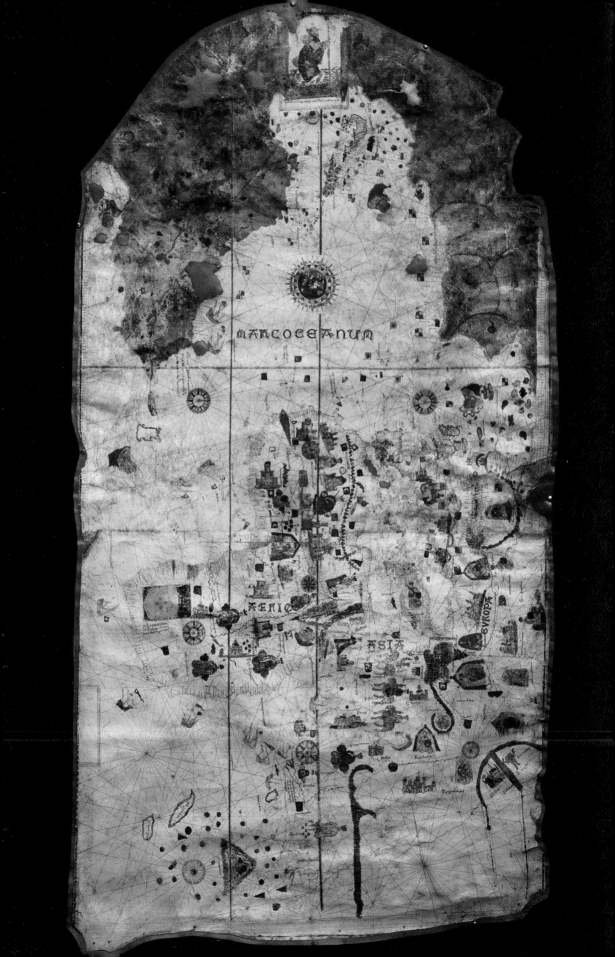

❧ FOUR ❧

A LIFE FORGOTTEN

1600-1699

S THE NEW CENTURY BEGAN, A BOOK WAS WRITTEN about the mysterious boat pilot who had revealed his secret to Columbus. The author, the Peruvian historian and librarian Garcilaso de la Vega, was the son of an Inca princess and a Spanish conquistador (soldier). He said that as a boy he had heard his father tell the story of the boat pilot to a neighbor. The father had even given the old pilot's name: Alonzo Sanchez. Supposedly Sanchez sailed from the Canary Islands "in 1484, one year more or less." The father claimed to even know how far this pilot Sanchez had sailed: to an island 750 leagues from the Canaries. There the pilot's ship was wrecked. Of the 17 crewmen aboard, only Sanchez survived—but he lived only long enough to make it back to Columbus's house, on the Portuguese island of Madeira, to reveal his secret to Columbus.

People in Spain were astounded by what the Peruvian historian had learned from his father. Surely, they thought, he must be telling

This map of the world, opposite, was drawn by Juan de la Cosa, who sailed with Columbus on his first two voyages. North is to the right and the Americas are at the top of the map. The inset picture at the top shows St. Christopher.

the truth, for he had so many "facts," and he sounded so sure of himself.

In the 1600s, other historians wrote about Columbus. But most of their books were travel books in which Columbus was mentioned along with many other explorers. Authors who did write about Columbus had little to say that was new or different from what early historians such as Peter Martyr had written years before.

As for the mystery of which island in the Bahamas Columbus first came to, no historian yet knew the answer. Columbus had named the island San Salvador. But in his journal he had not said exactly where it was and had left no map or chart of San Salvador. Spaniards had never settled there, although later they captured Indians from the island to use as workers in the colony on Hispaniola.

In 1625 a Spanish mapmaker claimed he had finally figured out the landfall—the first land Columbus sighted after the voyage. The mapmaker identified the place as the small island in the Bahamas called Cat. For the moment that seemed to end all discussion.

Another puzzle was not so easily solved. Since the 1500s, historians had been perplexed by the meaning of Columbus's peculiar signature. He had started signing his name that way after his first voyage. Only it was not really his name. Rather, it was a strange pyramid of letters that looked like this:

Columbus put this mysterious signature on about 50 letters or documents. He told his sons it was very important, but he never told them—or anyone else—what it meant.

No one had yet learned its secret. Historians suspected it had a religious meaning. Xp̄o FERENS are Greek and Latin words for Christ-bearer, which is what Cristoforo means in Italian.

But in the 17th century, ordinary people were not very interested in Columbus's signature, or anything else about him. What mattered to them were the lands he had found and the riches that these lands were producing for Spain. A steady stream of ships laden with silver and gold headed for Spain from colonies in the West Indies and Central and South America. For a time, Spain was the most wealthy and powerful country in Europe. Dozens of pirate ships from other parts of Europe now sailed the Spanish main—the Caribbean—to attack Spanish vessels for their precious cargoes.

In the 1600s, there were other ships on the high seas, too. English explorers sailed to both the east and west coasts of North America. Russian, Japanese, and Chinese vessels stopped along the west coast of North America. Shiploads of Spanish settlers flocked to the Spanish colonies in Central America, and Portuguese settlers sailed to Brazil.

Colonists began to settle in North America, too. The English started a colony at Jamestown. Although Spain had given up trying to control the northern part of its new empire, it kept what are now the states of New Mexico, Arizona, Texas, and California. And in 1620, English pilgrims landed on North America's Atlantic coast at Plymouth Rock.

These first settlers in the New World did not have time to think much about America's "discoverer." They had other problems—like trying to survive in a strange new land.

Columbus is shown in the act of landing and taking possession of the Indies in the name of Spain. A friar stands next him, carrying a crucifix, even though we know that no friars or priests sailed on the first voyage. Columbus is richly dressed and looks heroically untouched by the difficulties of the long voyage.

─── ❧ FIVE ❧ ───

SYMBOL FOR
A NEW NATION

1700-1799

N 1744, THE BIOGRAPHY OF CHRISTOPHER COLUMBUS
written by his son Ferdinand was translated into
English for the first time. Now even people who could
read only English could learn about the man who
discovered America.

In England, many people read the new translation of the Columbus biography. But in North America, most English colonists were
too busy to bother with a newly published book—even one about
Christopher Columbus. The colonists had other concerns. They
had land to clear, fields to plow, and businesses to run.

They soon had a war to fight as well. Alongside English soldiers,
the colonists battled French soldiers in what was known as the
French and Indian War. The fighting began in 1754 and lasted several years. Shortly after the war ended, England passed the Stamp
Act, which placed heavy taxes on the American colonies.

The colonists objected to the stamp tax and other taxes that followed. Before long, the colonies broke away from England. As the
people edged closer to forming a nation of their own, they needed a
new, non-English hero. And who better than Christopher Columbus, America's "discoverer"?

Immediately the colonists began naming things after Columbus.

A warship being built for the Continental Navy in 1775 was named *Columbus*. A magazine writer referred to the new nation-to-be as "Columbia."

And when the United States did become a nation, shipbuilders named other ships after Columbus, including the *Columbia Rediviva*, or "Columbia Reborn." This was the one Captain Robert Gray sailed from Boston on a voyage of exploration. Crewmen had shortened the name to *Columbia* by the time they rounded the tip of South America and made their way north to explore the Oregon territory. There, in 1792, Captain Gray discovered a river between present-day Oregon and Washington, which he named Columbia, after his ship and the nation's new hero.

By now people of the United States felt quite comfortable with Columbus as their hero. And because they felt theirs was a great nation, obviously its discoverer had to be great, too—a hero who was wise and brave, handsome and adventurous. Now was the time to read Ferdinand's biography of his father and take it to heart. Just as Ferdinand idolized a father who could do no wrong, so did the new citizens of the new United States of America.

Native Americans greeted Robert Gray when he "discovered" the Columbia River on his voyage of exploration to Oregon.

People called themselves "Columbians." Artists created an imaginary symbol of the nation, "Columbia," a woman dressed in flowing garments of red, white, and blue and carrying a shield decorated with stars and stripes. A new magazine called *The Columbian Magazine* was enormously popular.

In January of 1791, the founding fathers decided to put the nation's capital on land donated by the states of Virginia and Maryland. They would call the capital city Washington, after one of the nation's heroes. They named the land on which the city would be built the Territory of Columbia (later, District of Columbia), after America's other national hero, Columbus.

By the end of summer the following year, workmen in Washington were ready to build the White House, where the new nation's presidents would live. Officials made the men wait until October 12, 1792—300 years, to the day, after Columbus discovered America—to begin building. That day the nation's first president, George Washington, laid the first cornerstone for the White House—with a silver trowel.

The 300th anniversary of the discovery was a time of celebration in other cities, too. On October 12, 1792, the people of New York City marked Columbus Day for the first time. And on the same day, officials in Baltimore, Maryland, dedicated a monument to honor Columbus.

While people in the United States were spreading the name of America's discoverer from shore to shore, important activities related to Columbus were taking place in other countries. These had to do with the discovery of old artifacts, of old documents, and of old bones, and the solution—maybe—to an old Columbus mystery.

One day in 1781, in the part of Hispaniola occupied by the French, a colonial officer was watching workers dig a canal for a plantation. Then the workers stopped. One of them had discovered an ancient anchor. The officer, an amateur archaeologist, had been trying for some years to find the ruins of La Navidad. He guessed that the anchor was probably from Columbus's ship. He made sure it was saved and taken to a museum.

Two years later, in the part of Hispaniola that was still a Spanish colony, workmen were repairing the cathedral in Santo Domingo. The ancient building was now more than 250 years old and often in need of repair. It was where the small lead caskets containing the remains of Columbus, his son Diego, and his grandson Luis, had been buried since the 1500s.

The workmen came across a broken lead box containing human bones. One of the men remembered that on a repair job a few years before, he had seen a similar lead box with bones. But as near as he could recall, that box had been reburied on the other side of the altar. Or was it this side? No one was quite sure. No one was sure which box held the real Christopher Columbus, either. They reburied this second box as if it held the real remains.

The cathedral of Havana is officially dedicated to the Virgin of the Immaculate Conception, but it is better known as San Cristóbal. A box thought to contain Columbus's remains was buried in there in 1795.

A few years passed. Spain lost a war with France and in 1795 it had to give up its colony on Hispaniola. France now controlled the entire island, which was renamed Haiti. The duke of Veragua, a descendant of Columbus, did not believe the remains of his honored ancestor should be on "French republican" soil. He agreed to pay the cost of removing the small lead casket and reburying it in San Cristóbal, the cathedral of Havana in Cuba, which was still a Spanish colony.

Men set to work digging near the high altar of the Santo Domingo cathedral. They took out a lead box that they assumed held Columbus's remains. With solemn and elaborate ceremonies, the box was taken by ship to Cuba and reburied in the cathedral in Havana.

Meanwhile, across the Atlantic in Spain, a Spanish naval officer was collecting documents for a navy history he was writing. While going through papers in the library of a duke, the officer stumbled onto an amazing collection of documents. They included letters and reports written by Christopher Columbus himself, and a summary of Columbus's journal that had been written by Las Casas. These were papers that had been missing since the 1500s.

The navy project was dropped. What the officer had found was far more important. These documents would be of tremendous help to historians, but sorting them out would take time. The officer, whose name was Martín Fernández de Navarrete, had to read and recopy each document. Once he changed the old style of handwriting into a more modern way of writing, he had to translate the archaic Spanish, or the Latin, into modern Spanish. It was a tedious job that was to take him more than 30 years.

While the naval officer worked away, another Spanish historian was asked by the Spanish king to write a history of the New World. While doing his research, this historian reconsidered the landfall question and an old mystery: which island in the Bahamas was the first one to be discovered by Columbus?

The Bahamian chain of islands and cays stretches across the ocean southeast of Florida for over 500 miles (800 km). The historian

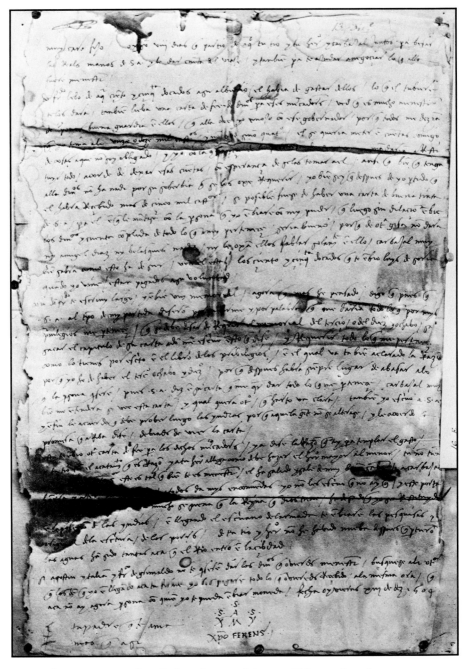

A letter written by Columbus to his son Diego, dated December 13, 1504

Where Was Columbus's First Landfall in the Americas?

ATLANTIC OCEAN

CAT ISLAND

SAN SALVADOR (WATLINGS ISLAND)

SAMANA CAY

MAYAGUANA

S. CAICOS

GRAND TURK (TURKS ISLAND)

BAHAMAS

CUBA

HISPANIOLA

NORTH AMERICA

SOUTH AMERICA

EQUATOR

BAHAMAS

puzzling over the mystery of the landfall believed he had found the answer. Since 1625, people had been sure the landfall was Cat, a narrow, boot-shaped island located near the middle of the long chain of Bahamian islands. But in 1793 the historian said he believed the landfall was a slightly larger island about 40 miles (65 km) southeast of Cat—the island called Watlings.

And so the 18th century ended with some new findings for historians to add to their ever-changing "story of Christopher Columbus": an anchor found in the West Indies and possibly from the *Santa María*, a whole treasure trove of Columbus documents discovered by a naval officer in Spain, the transfer of Columbus's remains from Santo Domingo to Cuba, and the answer to where Columbus first landed in the New World!

By the 1800s, Columbus was so much a symbol of United States history that he was even used to illustrate the title page of a history textbook.

❧ SIX ❧

COLUMBIA, THE GEM OF THE OCEAN

1800-1899

I N THE UNITED STATES, AS THE NEW CENTURY BEGAN, more towns were named for Columbus—Columbia, South Carolina, which became a town in 1805, and Columbia, Tennessee, first settled in 1807. Later came other Columbias in Connecticut, Illinois, Mississippi, Missouri, and four other states.

Columbus even had a rare new metal named in his honor. A scientist discovered the new metal in 1801 when he was studying a sample of ore that had been dug up in New England. The scientist called it columbium.

On patriotic holidays in the United States, the crowds could hear bands play a rousing new march, "Hail Columbia." The tune was old, but the words, by Joseph Hopkinson, were new. "Hail Columbia" was an immediate hit. People loved it and sang it often, as if it were their national anthem—something their country still did not have.

When the new nation again went to war with England, in 1812, the U.S. Army developed a new type of muzzle-loading cannon that it called the "Columbiad." And among the frigates, or warships, the navy had built one that it named *Columbia*.

During the War of 1812, some citizens of Canada and Nova Scotia sympathized with the United States. Since these northern lands were under British control, these sympathizers fled south across the border. Congress had bought some land for them in Ohio, and they settled in a new community that was called Columbus. An official explained that the town was given this name because "to him we are . . . indebted in being able to offer the refugees a resting place."

In Europe, the Columbus documents that the Spanish naval officer Navarrete had spent so much time translating into modern Spanish were finally published in 1825.

Besides Columbus's letters and journal notes, Navarrete's three volumes contained the writings of Diego Méndez. Méndez had been Columbus's majordomo, or right-hand man, and had sailed with Columbus on his fourth voyage. In his will, Méndez described that adventure, including his trip by canoe from Jamaica to Hispaniola to get help for the marooned Columbus and crew. Méndez made the 450-mile (724-km) journey with 13 other Spaniards and 20 Indians in two large canoes. Diego Méndez's writing went on for pages and pages. It provided historians with details about the fourth voyage not given in Ferdinand Columbus's *Historie* or in the letters Columbus wrote to the queen and king.

Navarrete also named his choice for the island where Columbus first landed. He said it was Grand Turk or Turks Island, a tiny island only a few miles square, located about 90 miles (145 km) from Hispaniola.

That stirred up again the arguments among historians about the true landfall. However, they were overjoyed to have the rest of the information that Navarrete had presented.

The American writer Washington Irving, who was in France in 1825, wanted to translate Navarrete's works into English. Irving went to Spain, only to find such a "mass of rich materials" that he decided to write his own history instead.

Irving did research in Spain's government archives, which had been opened to the public for the first time. He also went through papers in the private family archives of a Columbus descendant, the duke of Veragua. Fortunately Irving could read not only French, Spanish, and Italian, but also Latin.

Author Washington Irving helped make Columbus even more popular by writing the first American biography of him.

Next, Irving went to Palos on what he called "an American pilgrimage." He felt it was his "filial duty"—as a "son" of Columbus—to follow the path of Columbus before he set off on his first voyage to the New World.

"I cannot express," he said, "what my feelings were on trodding the shore which had once been animated with the bustle of departure and whose sands had been printed by the last footsteps of Columbus . . . like viewing the silent and empty stage of some great drama."

With two descendants of Martín Pinzón, Washington Irving also visited La Rábida, the monastery where Columbus took his young son Diego when they arrived in Spain for the first time.

The history of Columbus that Washington Irving wrote was published in 1828. Earlier, the popular writer had delighted readers with tales of a "headless horseman," Ichabod Crane, and Rip Van

Winkle. Now he gave his fans something special—the first biography published in America of their hero Columbus. For the next 50 or 60 years, Irving's history was the source of information for other writers doing books about Columbus. They accepted whatever he said about Columbus as true, although later historians would find that many of Irving's details about Columbus, including the birth date of 1435, were wrong.

Like Navarrete, Washington Irving plunged into what he called "the controversy of where Columbus landed." He disagreed with Navarrete's choice of Turks Island. Irving pointed out that in Columbus's journal, Columbus described the landfall island as level, with fresh water, and covered with forests and fruit trees. Turks did

A dramatic sketch of the "egg story." Columbus stands back from the table, pointing to the egg he has balanced on the front right corner.

not fit this description, said Irving, for Turks was "sand and rocks" and had no fresh water. Irving agreed with earlier historians who had selected Cat Island as the landfall. Some of Irving's fellow historians in Europe praised his choice.

In his book about Columbus, Washington Irving repeated the famous "egg story" that had appeared in earlier histories of Columbus. Irving felt the story had to be true, because it had been retold so often. Supposedly Columbus attended a dinner party at which several Spanish noblemen argued that anyone could have made the discovery that Columbus made. To answer them, Columbus took an egg. He asked who among them could make it stand on end. None could. Then Columbus crushed one end of the egg just enough to keep it upright.

"After the deed is done," he explained, "everyone knows how to do it!"

Irving's *History of the Life and Voyages of Christopher Columbus* was published at a time when people of the United States still felt very close to their discoverer. Along with the new biography of Columbus, people had another patriotic song honoring him: David Shaw's "Columbia, the Gem of the Ocean." And in New York an editor for the *Herald Tribune* even proposed in an editorial in 1846 that "our country shall take to herself the name Columbia in honor of the great Discoverer of this Continent."

As the nation debated building a railroad across the continent, politicians praised the idea. They said locomotives would pick up where Columbus's sailing ships had left off. The United States, with a railroad from coast to coast, would become the link between Europe and Asia.

In 1849, the rush for gold began. And when the citizens of California named their new state's capital city, the name they chose was Columbia.

By the late 1800s, some people in the United States had come to almost worship Columbus as superhuman and bigger than life. Joaquin Miller, a poet of the American West, wrote of a brave Columbus who faced his frightened and mutinous crew on that first

Romantic portraits of Columbus abounded. Left, in an engraving from a book of the late 1800s, he points to land as his crew marvels. Right, a mournful and tragic Columbus is shipped back to Spain in heavy chains.

voyage and told them, "Sail on! Sail on! Sail on! And on!" For many citizens of the United States, these words became a life's motto. Sidney Lanier, a poet from Georgia, wrote of frightened crewmen who wanted to turn back, and of Columbus who ordered his steersman to "hold straight into the West."

To many, Christopher Columbus became a symbol of the westward movement in the United States in the 19th century. Columbus had sailed west from Spain to claim new lands for his queen (without regard, as later historians would point out, for the native peoples' claim to the property). Now, in the 1800s, pioneers were heading across the plains in prairie "schooners" to seek land where they could homestead and settle down—carrying the discoveries of Columbus forward across the continent.

Writers in Europe also began to see Columbus as a romantic hero. One historian, a French count, felt Columbus was so good and noble that he should be made a saint!

Then, quite abruptly, a few books appeared that were less kind to Columbus. A German historian in 1866 pointed out that the Norsemen were the first discoverers of America. Obviously, he said, Columbus was only the "rediscoverer." In 1874 another writer, who had only contempt for "the so-called Columbus," repeated that old, old story about the dying boat pilot with the secret.

Soon after this debate was reopened, workmen in the West Indies made a startling discovery. While they were repairing the aging Santo Domingo cathedral in 1877, they found a lead box near the vault from which "Columbus's remains" had been removed almost 100 years earlier. Inside the box were bones and ashes. Church authorities rushed to inspect what they had found. And etched in

This is the lead box containing bones—perhaps those of Columbus—found in the Santo Domingo cathedral in 1877. The engraving on the lid is just visible.

the lid and on the bottom of the box were words that seemed to indicate the remains were those of "the illustrious and excellent man Don Cristóval Colón"—Christopher Columbus! But how could that be? Hadn't Columbus's remains been taken to Cuba in 1795? While workers and churchmen examined the box, some of the ashes from it fell to the floor. Portions of these ashes, it has been said, later turned up as "Columbus relics" in New York and in three cities in Italy.

And what did the surprising discovery of the lead box mean? To the people of Cuba, it meant that whoever was buried in the Havana cathedral was probably not Columbus. To the people of Santo Domingo, it meant that the bones of Columbus had never left their island after all. Immediately, plans were made to build an elaborate marble monument in the Santo Domingo cathedral to properly honor the burial place of these recently discovered bones of Columbus. (By this time the bones were no longer on French soil. Haiti had given up the eastern half of the island of Hispaniola and that half had become Santo Domingo and later became the Dominican Republic.)

With the discovery of Columbus's missing bones, the excitement and confusion continued in the West Indies. To the north, the people of the United States were too busy promoting Columbus Day to pay much attention.

In 1889 the Catholic fraternal group, Knights of Columbus, campaigned to have the day of Columbus's discovery declared a legal holiday. In San Francisco, people had already been celebrating "Discovery Day" each October 12 for 20 years, with floats and pageants and a reenactment of the first landing. And across the country, schoolchildren had been celebrating the holiday for years—legal or not. On October 12, youngsters marched in parades, drew pictures of the brave admiral, and made models of his three ships.

The holiday was not made legal in 1889, as its promoters had hoped. But as the United States prepared to celebrate the 400th anniversary of Columbus's landing, President Benjamin Harrison declared October 12, 1892, a general holiday for everyone. The president urged the people to "cease from toil" on that day, and to devote themselves "to exercises to honor Christopher Columbus."

As the years went by, people in the Americas went on naming things in honor of Columbus—or Cristóbal Colón, as the Latin Americans called him. Cities, towns, counties, and provinces from Canada to the tip of South America were named for him. Americans gave his name to rivers, lakes, islands, mountains, and schools— from Mount Columbia in the Canadian Rockies to Colón, Argentina, and from Columbia University in New York City to Cristóbal in the Canal Zone and Colón, Cuba. Late in the 1800s the South American country of New Granada was renamed the United States of Colombia.

By the end of the century, town squares, museums, schoolrooms, and meeting halls throughout the Americas had statues and paintings of Christopher Columbus. In the United States his portrait hung in the capitol in Washington, D.C., and in the U.S. Naval

The porcelain statue on the left is based on the monument to Columbus in Mexico City, Mexico. The monument on the right stands in front of Columbus City Hall in Columbus, Ohio.

Academy. Philadelphia had a statue of Columbus, paid for by Italian citizens of that city. In New York City, a statue of Columbus marked the southwest entrance to Central Park, called Columbus Circle.

Surprisingly, as late as 1890 there was still no monument to mark the spot where Columbus first set foot on American soil. The *Chicago Herald*, looking ahead to celebrations planned for 1892, decided to erect a monument. The problem was which island to choose. Of the 29 islands and 661 cays in the Bahamas, five had been suggested so far: Cat, Watlings, Grand Turk, Mayaguana, and Samana. Samana Cay was the choice of Gustavus Fox, who had been assistant secretary of the navy under President Abraham Lincoln. Fox had made a government survey in the area that was published in 1882.

The *Chicago Herald* sent an expedition to settle the question. They finally chose Watlings as the site for their monument. Ten other newspapers objected and offered suggestions of their own. Despite the protests, the monument was built on Watlings, just in time for the big 400th anniversary celebration in 1892.

To the government of the United States, the 400th anniversary of

A cross and plaque stand at the spot on Watlings Island that was believed to mark Columbus's first landfall in the Americas.

The Main Basin of the Columbian Exposition reflects the electric lights that lit up the grounds at night. Visitors were dwarfed by the statue of Columbus at the entrance to the fairgrounds.

Columbus's discovery was so special that the nation hosted a world exposition, or fair, in Jackson Park, Chicago. When the Columbian Exposition finally opened in May 1893, visitors marveled at all there was to see and do. They were astounded by new inventions, such as the electric light bulbs that lit up the buildings and walkways by night. This exposition was the first to have a midway—a separate area with rides and other entertainments that included "hootchy-kootchy" dancers from Egypt and Buffalo Bill and his Wild West Show.

Looming majestically over the crowds as they entered the fairgrounds was a huge statue of Columbus. Sword in one hand, Spanish flag in the other, he was depicted "taking possession of America."

These are just a few of the ways artists have pictured Columbus.

The fair featured a full-sized reproduction of the Spanish monastery of La Rábida where Columbus had visited so often. Although no artist had drawn or painted a portrait of Columbus in his lifetime — nor for many years after he died — in the monastery replica were 71 portraits of Columbus that were claimed to be authentic. Some showed him with a beard and mustache, others had him clean-shaven. There were fat faces, thin faces, Columbuses with dark

The gallery at the exposition had versions of many of these portraits.

complexions, Columbuses with pale skin. No two were alike. What Columbus wore often reflected the clothing of the century in which the artist painted the picture. Judges were appointed to choose the most accurate likeness of Christopher Columbus, but they gave up trying to decide which it might be.

Also in the monastery building, protected day and night by armed soldiers, were Columbus relics lent by the pope, the government of

Spain, and Columbus's descendants. There were letters Columbus had written, an original copy of his agreement with the Spanish sovereigns, and an anchor and cannon he had used.

But the Columbus relics that fascinated fair-goers most were life-size copies of his ships—the *Santa María* and the caravels *Niña* and *Pinta*. All three had been built in Spain and sailed to Chicago's waterfront on Lake Michigan by way of Watlings Island in the Bahamas, New York, and the St. Lawrence River.

Another big hit of the fair was a photograph of a little boy standing by the sea. It was called "Child Columbus." The fact that it could not possibly be a photograph of Columbus as a child did not seem to bother admiring fair-goers.

What may have bothered some, however, was the replica of a ninth-century Viking ship. Captain Magnus Andersen and his crew of 35 had sailed the ship in 28 days from Bergen, Norway, to Newfoundland. Then they had sailed on to the fair to boost the theory that Norsemen discovered America in 1001, some 400 years before Columbus.

The Columbian Exposition was a spectacular way to honor Christopher Columbus and to end the century. But even before the fair opened, something far more important to Columbus scholars happened. Looking forward to the anniversary celebration, the Italian government had commissioned a Columbus scholar to collect all of the existing Columbus material. The result was a 14-volume publication called the *Raccolta* (the short title for a very long Italian title that began: "*Raccolta de documenti...*"). The *Raccolta* was published between 1892 and 1896. Some of the Columbus documents had been discovered recently. Others were new translations of old documents. The *Raccolta* printed transcripts of the court hearings from the early 1500s in Spain, the hundreds of notes that Columbus and his brother Bartholomew had written in the margins of books they owned, and notary records from the 1400s concerned with the Colombo family.

As soon as the *Raccolta* was published, historians began writing books about Columbus based on the new information. More books

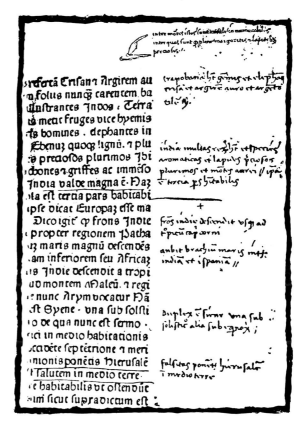

This section of a page from one of Columbus's books shows his habit of underlining and making comments to himself in the margin.

about Columbus would come later, in the 20th century, after scholars and historians had more time to sort through all of the material.

At the very end of the 19th century, two important ceremonies took place. The first was at the cathedral of Havana in Cuba. Cuba had just become independent. That meant the ex-colony was no longer Spanish soil, so the lead casket that some still believed contained Columbus's bones was taken from its place of honor in the cathedral. The casket was returned to Spain where, with another elaborate ceremony, it was interred in a magnificent, newly built tomb in the Seville cathedral.

But the question haunted historians: Were the bones in Spain those of Columbus—or were his bones still back at the cathedral in Santo Domingo?

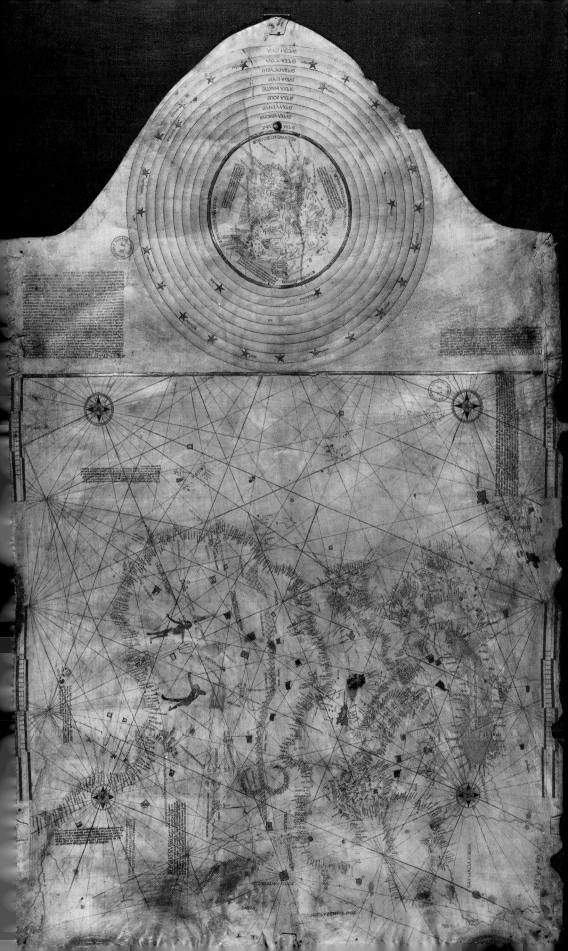

SEVEN

REEXAMINING THE EVIDENCE

1900-1992

S THE 20TH CENTURY BEGAN, HISTORIANS WERE STILL studying the *Raccolta*. Sorting through all of the documents and papers, they began to gain a much better idea of Columbus's plans and ambitions. And they were able to solve some puzzling questions about his early years.

The reason historians had known so little about Columbus's early years was because he didn't say much about them. It would have helped if Columbus had had a driver's license—but in his day, there was no such thing. Nor were there census takers. There were few written records of any sort in the mid-1400s, since most people could not read or write. And no birth certificates or baptismal records were kept for an ordinary family like the Colombos. So historians had little evidence to tell them about Columbus's parents, or when he was born and where he lived, or if he went to school, or what his first job was.

The map opposite is supposed to be one used by Columbus on his first trip to the Americas. Much of the coast of Africa had been explored by then, but the New World does not appear on the map. The round inset at the top shows the old theory of the universe: Earth is at the center, and everything else revolves around it.

Fortunately, in Columbus's day there were notaries. Notaries, who could read and write Latin, took care of certain legal transactions, just as a lawyer does today. People went to the notary when they wanted to make a will, agree to a contract with someone, or settle a debt or an argument. Members of the Colombo family probably went to a notary often, but only about two dozen notary records have been located. Most were printed in the *Raccolta* in 1892 and some have been found since then.

Historians were able to match Columbus's own statements about being "of Genoa" with evidence from notary records. One record, for example, was about payment for a shipment of sugar. It listed Columbus as a witness to the transaction, referring to him as "Christopher Columbus, citizen of Genoa." Other notary records established that Domenico Colombo was a weaver who lived near a certain gate in Genoa. Still other records listed Domenico as father of Christopher. This helped historians decide Columbus was not from Spain, Corsica, England, Portugal, or any of the other places that claimed him as their native son, and that he was the son of a weaver.

To establish Columbus's age, historians matched information from two different notary documents. In a document dated August 25, 1479, Columbus was mentioned and his age was given as "about 27 years." Another notary record about money Domenico Colombo owed referred to "Cristoforo Colombo, son of Domenico," and described him as "an adult 19 years of age." That document was dated October 31, 1470.

From these two pieces of evidence, historians could figure Columbus's birth date. If Columbus was 19 on October 31, 1470, and he was 27 on August 25, 1479, his birth date had to be between August 25, 1451 and October 31, 1451. In books about Columbus today, the birth date is usually given as "between August and October, 1451," or "in the fall of 1451."

No early records have been found noting the birth of Columbus's brothers and sister or their names. Even so, historians were able to find out this information by studying notary records carefully. One notary record in the *Raccolta* told of the sale of a house by the

Colombos and mentioned "Susanna, wife of Domenico" and their sons "Cristoforo and Giovanni Pellegrino." This confirmed that Columbus's mother's name was Susanna, and it told historians that, besides Diego and Bartholomew, Christopher Columbus had a brother named Giovanni Pellegrino. Another document in the *Raccolta* had to do with a woman named Bianchinetta, whose husband, a cheese maker, had sued his father-in-law, Domenico Colombo, for a promised dowry. Since historians knew that Domenico was Columbus's father, they figured out that Bianchinetta had to be Columbus's sister.

The *Raccolta* reprinted many of the notes that Columbus and his brother Bartholomew wrote in the margins of their books later in life when they were both adults (and Christopher could read). From these comments, or *postil*, in the margins of the books, historians learned what Columbus thought about things, and what he hoped to find on his first voyage.

Of course, not every new Columbus document that turned up in the late 1800s and early 1900s was helpful to historians. One famous hoax was the "letter in a barrel." On his return to Spain, back in 1493, Columbus had tossed the barrel with a letter sealed inside into the stormy sea. He planned that even if his ship went down, his letter might reach the queen and king. But his ship did not sink, and the letter and barrel were never seen again. Years later, Columbus's son Ferdinand offered a reward of 1,000 ducats for the return of the barrel and its letter. Ferdinand got no takers. And for the next 400 years, nothing was heard of the barrel or the letter. Then a man claimed he had found the letter on the seacoast of Wales in southwest England. He said it had "washed ashore" in 1893. It was written in English. "Easier to read," the seller explained. Since Columbus did not know English, this certainly cast doubt on the story!

Sometimes figuring out whether a document was forged was not so easy. In 1902 the duchess of Alba and Berwick, a Columbus descendant, bought a damaged notebook and map from a private owner. They seemed genuine, but historians had no way of knowing for sure.

This photo from the Library of Congress is identified as "The famous Columbus tree at Santo Domingo, Dominican Republic. It was to this tree that Columbus is said to have moored his caravel, when he landed on American soil." This must be another Columbus hoax—or else the water was much deeper next to the shore in 1492!

Historians also had doubts about certain documents printed in the *Raccolta*. How could they be sure they weren't forged? In some cases, the historians consulted graphologists—experts at analyzing handwriting—who studied the documents and declared them authentic.

Despite the handwriting experts, a historian named Henry Vignaud accused Columbus's son Ferdinand and the historian Las Casas of writing some notes in the margins of Columbus's books themselves. He also claimed that Columbus did not have plans to seek the Indies when he began his voyage, but that Ferdinand and Las Casas had doctored Columbus's journal to make it sound as if those were his plans.

Above, a part of the Archives of the Indies at Seville. Right, Alice Bache Gould as a young woman. These archives are where Gould began her long project of learning about Columbus's crewmen.

Later historians proved Henry Vignaud wrong.

In 1911, an American woman named Alice Bache Gould made a surprising discovery. She was doing research at the Archives of the Indies in Seville when she came across the name of a man who had gone on one of Columbus's voyages—or so historians thought. But the information Gould found proved he had not. Her discovery gave her an idea. Why not compile a list of all of Columbus's shipmates on that first voyage? No one had done this before.

Alice Gould devoted the next 40 years of her life to the project. Besides names, she learned all sorts of other useful facts about the crewmen—where they came from, what they did aboard ship, what wages they earned. Thanks to her, historians learned much about

In the early 20th century, New York's Museum of the American Indian sponsored archaeological digs to uncover remains of the Arawak Indians in the Caribbean.

the voyages that they hadn't known before. The American historian and Columbus scholar Samuel Eliot Morison praised Alice Gould's work as "the most valuable piece of Columbian research in the present [20th] century."

Besides Alice Gould, other historians were still doing research in Europe. By the 1930s, however, many historians turned their attention to the Caribbean. They felt they had explored nearly every hiding place in Europe looking for Columbus material. In the Caribbean there was still much to learn. Archaeologists could look for other Columbus artifacts, like the anchor from the *Santa María* that was discovered in Hispaniola. They could hunt for the ruins of La Navidad, the fort Columbus had built with lumber from the wrecked *Santa María*.

Historian Samuel Morison, who was also an admiral and a sailor, decided to go where Columbus had sailed, and "to view the islands and coasts as through his eyes." One winter in the 1930s, Morison chartered a yawl and sailed the route of Columbus's second voyage through the Caribbean.

Later Morison and a crew that was partly from Harvard University formed The Harvard Columbus Expedition. In several ships, they crossed the Atlantic, tracing the routes of his historic voyages. Morison also tried, without success, to locate the ruins of La Navidad. He did believe, however, that he had found where Columbus first

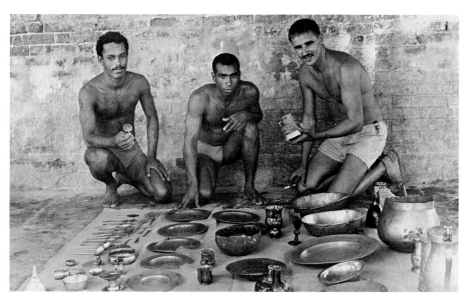

Robert Marx (right) displays some of the items found in one of his underwater archaeological explorations off the coast of Jamaica. Many Spanish ships were sunk in the waters of the Caribbean.

landed. He agreed with several other historians who claimed the landfall was an island now called San Salvador, but once known as Watlings.

Samuel Morison wrote several books about Columbus, including the biography *Admiral of the Ocean Sea*, which won a Pulitzer Prize in 1943. His advice to historians was to do library research and then "go out and see for yourself."

In 1962 the marine archaeologist Robert Marx did just that. Marx was co-organizer and navigator of the expedition of the *Niña II*. The ship was a replica of Columbus's tiny caravel. To experience conditions Columbus had sailed under, Marx and his crew wore the sort of clothing Columbus's men probably wore. Their ship's cook used a firebox on deck to prepare the same kind of food Columbus's crews would have eaten. And since forks were not used in the 15th century, these 20th-century adventurers ate with knives, spoons, and their fingers.

In the early 1960s, Samuel Morison found another way to do Columbus research: by airplane. While in South America to give a lecture to the Colombian navy, Morison went flying with his translator, Mauricio Obregon, in Obregon's small plane. This gave the two men the idea of using an airplane to trace the routes of explorers. As Obregon explained in an interview, "You can go high and get a maplike view, and low for the view of a sailor up a mast." Morison and Obregon did fly around the Caribbean in a small plane, with photographers to take pictures. The result was a book the two men wrote together called *The Caribbean as Columbus Saw It*.

In 1949, a few years before Morison and Obregon began their collaboration, another pilot had flown over Haiti taking aerial photographs. One picture he took near Cap Haitien showed an oval-shaped blur. He wondered if the blur was an underwater reef that had formed over the lost *Santa María*.

Six years later, Edwin Link, inventor of the Link Trainer and an amateur marine archaeologist, searched the area. He found another anchor. Probably it, too, was from the *Santa María*, since Link found it not far from where the first one had been found 200 years earlier.

Marine archaeologist Fred Dickson also explored the area. After studying Columbus's journal entries for that Christmas Eve in 1492 when the *Santa María* was wrecked, Dickson and his team attempted four underwater "digs." One time they found a copper bolt and washer. Later, they discovered other artifacts, including a piece of broken pottery. Metal specialists who later examined the bolt and washer found them "consistent with 15th-century copper products." Experts at the Smithsonian Institution in Washington tested the pottery to determine when it was made. They fixed the date between 1375 and 1575. So it, too, could have come from the *Santa María*!

Despite other unsuccessful attempts to locate La Navidad, in 1982 archaeologists from the University of Florida found evidence of the town near La Navidad where the Arawak Indians had lived. Besides Indian artifacts, the archaeologists found pieces of glass. That could mean the Arawaks of this lost town had traded with Europeans—

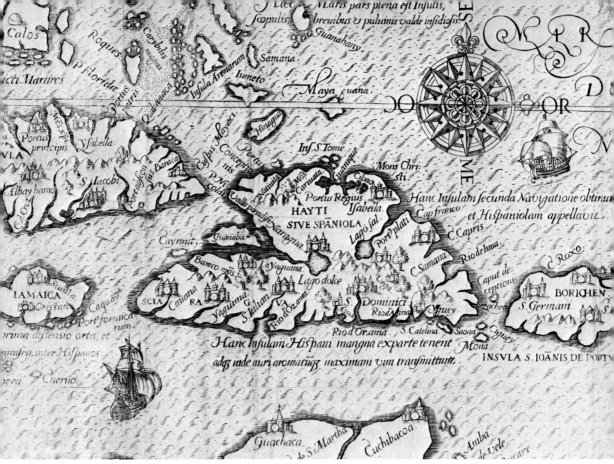

This 1594 map shows the Spanish settlements on Hispaniola (the island labelled "Hayti Sive Spaniola"). La Navidad is "Nativita" on the northwest corner of the island. Historians have always known approximately where the settlement was built, but they have not yet been able to find its exact location.

possibly crewmen from the *Santa María*, or sailors who had gone there afterward. It would have to have been soon after, because a short time after Columbus's first visit all of the Arawaks were gone. They had died from measles or smallpox epidemics, from overwork in the fields and gold mines of the colonists on Hispaniola, from starvation, from suicide, or in battles with the Spanish.

In their digs, archaeologists found the ruins of a well with a pig tooth and a rat bone inside. Columbus had written in his journal of coming back to La Navidad on his second voyage, and of looking into the ruins of a well. He had hoped to find gold that might have been hidden by the men who remained at the fort and were later killed. The well found by the archaeologists may have been the one Columbus mentioned in his journal.

A scientist analyzed the tooth and bone to determine their ages. He concluded that the tooth came from a Seville pig, and that the bone came from an Old World rat. That meant the animals must have come to the New World on a Spanish ship, possibly one of Columbus's.

By the last decades of the 1900s, historians knew enough about Columbus to shatter many myths and legends that had charmed earlier generations. Twentieth-century historians knew that many other educated people besides Columbus realized the world was round, and that he did not make his voyage to prove the fact. They knew that Spain did not have to empty its jails to provide a crew for that first voyage, as romantic poets had once suggested. And by now historians had explained away the myth that Queen Isabella had to pawn her jewels to pay for the voyage. The story got started because someone long ago misread Ferdinand Columbus and the historian Bartolomé de Las Casas, who wrote that the queen was "willing to pawn her jewels." Isabella never had to, because the royal treasurer said he would lend his own money instead.

Also, Columbus did not die penniless, as people once believed. This myth probably got started because Las Casas had written that Columbus died "impecunious [poor] and in a state of great misery." Miserable Columbus may have been, for he was old and sick, and he believed the Crown had cheated him. But he was not penniless. He had been collecting revenues from gold mines in Hispaniola for 10 years. By the standards of his day, he was a wealthy man.

Historian Samuel Morison disproved the story about Columbus and the egg. Said Morison, "a self-made admiral" at such a banquet would have better things to do than "juggle a hard-boiled egg." He pointed out that the same story had appeared earlier in books about other famous Italians.

Historians had learned quite a lot about Columbus. Even so, there were questions still unanswered—the meaning of his strange signature, for one. Most historians believed it was related to his Catholic religion. Others claimed the signature proved that Columbus was Portuguese, or that he belonged to the secret society of

Freemasons. A United States engineer in the 1980s had a different idea. He suggested the strange signature was a map. He said Columbus was proud of his discoveries, and this was how he pinpointed the islands in the Caribbean where he made his first landings.

Another mystery as yet unsolved was the light Columbus saw the night before his fleet reached land on October 12, 1492. In his

In this artist's imagining, Columbus's crew reacts to the mysterious light in the west with amazement and wonder. Although Columbus claimed the reward for being the first to spot land, in fact all he saw was this light. It was another sailor who, a few hours later, was the first to actually see land.

journal Columbus wrote that at about 10 o'clock at night he saw "a light to the west . . . like a little wax candle rising and falling." This had puzzled historians throughout the centuries. One theory was that the light was from fires the natives had built to "discourage sand fleas," although several critics pointed out that Columbus was 28 miles (45 km) away—too far to have seen such fires on the island. A more recent theory was that the light was from batches of tiny, luminescent—or glowing—worms on the surface of the water.

Just as that light to the west remains a puzzle, so does the question of where Columbus first landed.

In 1926 officials in the Bahamas were so sure the landfall was Watlings that they had changed the name of that island to San Salvador, the name Columbus gave to the island where he first came ashore. (The Arawaks knew it as Guanahaní.) Although Watlings—now called San Salvador—had four monuments marking it as the landfall, some people were not convinced. They went on searching for the *real* San Salvador.

In 1947 a Dutch seaman and navigator named Pieter Verhoog wrote a booklet, *Guanahaní Again*, in which he claimed that Columbus had first landed at South Caicos Island. Verhoog figured out where the landfall was by plotting a sea chart based on the sailing directions in Columbus's journal. Verhoog's book revived interest in the landfall question. While Edwin Link was doing underwater exploring in the Caribbean in 1955, he and his party, traveling by both airplane and boat, also tried to retrace the route Columbus might have followed to that first landfall.

In 1981 the National Geographic Society sponsored a study to find where Columbus first landed. The director of that study, *National Geographic* magazine's senior associate editor, Joseph Judge, put together a team of mathematicians, archaeologists, mapmakers, navigators, and others. To aid in the search, computer experts retranslated Columbus's journal line by line. With a computer program they called CRT (Columbus Research Tool), they plotted various routes, taking into account currents and a ship's sideways slip due to the wind. Then they "sailed" the course by electronics.

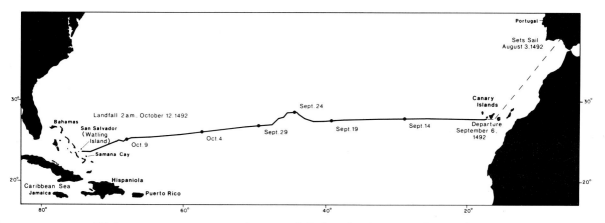

This computer-generated map of Columbus's route shows the course plotted by the Woods Hole Oceanographic Institute's team. The Woods Hole team placed Columbus's landing on San Salvador.

It took the *National Geographic* team of experts five years to locate what they believed was the right island. In 1986 Joseph Judge announced it was Samana Cay.

After he made his announcement, the *National Geographic* editor told a reporter he was "98 percent sure" Samana Cay was where Columbus landed. The only "infallible proof" would be the original Columbus log and chart—lost long ago.

But only one year later another team of scientists, this time from Woods Hole Oceanographic Institute in Massachusetts, joined the debate over the Columbus landfall. They, too, used a computer-generated track with corrections for winds and currents. Their calculations pointed back to San Salvador Island.

And so the controversy continued as the world prepared to celebrate the 500th anniversary of Columbus's voyage in 1992.

This metal bust was cast in Genoa in 1892. At the base is Columbus's coat of arms, granted him by the sovereigns of Spain. On top of the arms are the castle and lion, symbols of the royal families of Castile and Leon, and below are islands and anchors, symbols of the Admiral of the Ocean Sea.

✤ EIGHT ✤

YEAR OF
"THE QC JUBILEE"
1992

N 1985, THE UNITED STATES CONGRESS PASSED THE Christopher Columbus Quincentenary Jubilee Act. Right away a commission started planning a big celebration for 1992. But Quincentenary, which means 500th anniversary, was a real tongue twister. Whenever they could, jubilee planners called it "QC" instead.

Soon after the jubilee commission was formed, teams of historians and translators in the Americas and in Europe began work on QC projects. Italian scholars were making up-to-date translations (into Italian) of documents from the original *Raccolta* of 1892, and of any Columbus papers found since then, for a *Nuova Raccolta*. Scholars in Spain and at the University of California in Los Angeles were preparing *Repertorium Columbianum* ("RC" for short). It will contain English translations of many of the court hearings from the early 1500s and other Columbus source materials. Another important part of the RC will be a translation into English of the *Aztec Chronicles*, an old manuscript in Nahuatl, the Aztec language, that tells of the lives of early Native Americans. Modern historians recognize that the people who greeted Columbus in "the Indies" in 1492 had a history and heritage that was largely destroyed by the Spaniards.

The way historians now tell the Columbus story is very different from the way they told his story a century earlier. Historians in 1892 celebrated the discoverer, but most of them completely ignored the discovered. Historians are now trying to present a more balanced version. Instead of saying Columbus "discovered a new world," they speak of "a meeting of two worlds, both old." Native Americans had lived on the continent for thousands of years before Columbus arrived. The world that Columbus came to was just as "old" as the one he had left a few weeks before. As many Native Americans today are quick to point out, "We knew who *we* were, because we were here—it was Christopher Columbus who was discovered!"

They might have added that Columbus was not the first European to come to America anyway. Long before he came, there were the Norsemen—although they did not stay. And the Norsemen were

Columbus Circle, New York City, which contains a statue of Columbus on the pedestal, is an important crossroads in the city.

not the first people to visit, either. Perhaps 20,000 years before Viking ships reached America's shores, the ancestors of the Indians had probably come to North America by way of present-day Alaska.

Even though Christopher Columbus was not the first European to come to America, it was he who got the holiday, not to mention all those things named in his honor—ships, towns, rivers, songs, and, in the 20th century, a movie studio, a radio broadcasting company, and one of the astronauts' space shuttles. By 1990, Congress even considered legislation to have a new gold-colored copper one-dollar coin with the likeness of Columbus. And citizens of the District of Columbia were already planning for the day when their district would become the state of Columbia.

As the year of the QC approached, the jubilee committee made plans for television specials, parades, art shows, and school programs. Nautical buffs got ready to sail from Spain to the Americas in sailing

A reconstruction of the Santa María *under full sail*

Hispaniola was once forested and un-polluted. This bay of the Dominican Republic still is today, but much of the island now is bare and eroded, like this Haitian farmland below.

ships of every size. Some would even make the journey in replicas of the ships in Columbus's first tiny fleet.

Before the anniversary year itself, scholars and scientists from all parts of the world came to the Americas to meet and exchange information. At conferences on the environment, botanists and other scientists talked about plants and animals of the West Indies that became extinct after the Spanish came. Other experts spoke about the effects of deforestation—the reckless cutting down of trees by early colonists and later populations. A serious concern of today's environmentalists is how the world's climate will suffer if too many trees are cut down. Similarly, Columbus, who was a shrewd observer of the natural world, once wrote that while he was anchored off

A ball court on Puerto Rico, below, and gold ornaments from Costa Rica. These are among the few pre-Columbian artifacts and structures remaining.

Jamaica during his fourth voyage he noticed that rain fell every afternoon. He recalled that in the Canary Islands it used to rain every afternoon in just the same pattern. After people on the Canary Islands cut down all of the trees, he remembered that the afternoon rains no longer came down as hard, or as often.

Along with conferences held in the 1990s, experts in anthropology and archaeology studied Indian tribes at the time of Columbus and after. They tried to figure out the tribal boundaries, learn something of the cultures, and learn how the tribes related to each other. They looked for evidence of the beautiful gold jewelry and ornaments of some vanished cultures of Latin America, although nearly all of these valuable treasures and ornaments were taken to Spain and melted down during the 16th and 17th centuries.

Scholars attending conferences as the QC approached searched for evidence of history from the point of view of the native peoples. For example, Columbus wrote that natives in the Indies "know of no sect whatever." Since they were not Christians or Jews, nor did they belong to any of the other religions that Columbus knew, he did not recognize their beliefs. Other early colonists and explorers did write about the various religious practices of different groups of Native Americans. Even though most of the signs of Arawak life on the Caribbean islands were destroyed by the colonists, some artifacts and evidence have survived. For example, archaeologists have found carved figures that they believe were used in religious ceremonies.

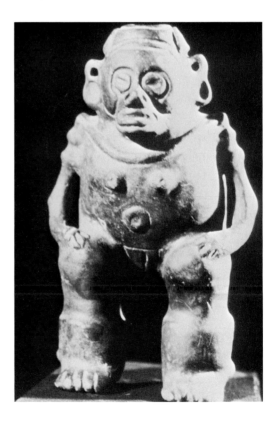

This round clay figure represents a Taino god. A few other carved or clay symbols of the Taino religion have been found.

This early wood-cut of Arawaks shows one of their inventions that was gladly accepted by the Europeans: the hammock.

Many people who attended conferences connected with the QC wrote books about their findings. Some historians wrote of the darker side to the arrival of Columbus and the Europeans who followed. For example, along with horses, the Spanish also brought germs. Natives, who were not immune to smallpox and measles and other European diseases, died by the thousands. These diseases, combined with starvation, forced labor, warfare, suicide, and torture and other forms of maltreatment by the Spanish, reduced the Indian population very rapidly. On Hispaniola, the original native population has been estimated to be about 250,000 to 300,000 in 1492. By 1548, Oviedo reported that only about 500 were left.

Among the new Columbus books for adults and young people published in the last decades of the 20th century were books about Columbus's ancestors, and about his life and travels before he made that famous voyage to America. There were books that retold the old familiar story of Columbus's voyages. One author suggested

Columbus was Portuguese, and of noble blood. Another writer theorized that Columbus was a Jew, and his voyage was a desperate search for a homeland for Jews driven from Spain in 1492.

Just in time for the QC year, there were also ideas for solving that 200-year-old mystery: Where are Columbus's bones? The expert who

Columbus arrives again on the Dominican Republic in this present-day pageant to celebrate Columbus Day.

had tested the bone and tooth samples taken from the archaeological digs in La Navidad now turned to testing tooth enamel taken from the Columbus remains in the cathedral of Santo Domingo. By analyzing the composition of the teeth, the scientist believed he could establish whether or not the bones in Santo Domingo were those of Columbus.

Ignoring such advanced methods for solving the mystery, a Spanish authority from Seville said the solution was simple. Columbus's bones were divided up. Part were in the cathedral in Seville, and part were in the cathedral in Santo Domingo, in what is now the Dominican Republic.

Meanwhile, in Santo Domingo, which is the capital city of the Dominican Republic, civic and religious leaders continue to hold an elaborate ceremony each October 12. That is the one day during the year when the public can view the casket containing what the Dominicans claim are the real Christopher Columbus bones.

With the bone mystery not completely settled, schoolchildren still go on celebrating Columbus Day in the same way they always have. In Santiago, Chile—where, as in the rest of Latin America, the day is called *Día de la Raza*, or Day of the Race—toddlers at nursery schools paint three cardboard boxes like miniature replicas of the *Santa María*, *Niña*, and *Pinta*, and then climb into their "ships" and move across a stage to reenact Columbus's first voyage. Older students in El Salvador and Guatemala and other countries march in parades. At schools in the United States, students make models of the three ships of Columbus and draw pictures of the Admiral. But throughout the Western Hemisphere, schoolchildren also do projects that help them understand more about the Indies that Columbus found. They study native cultures. They learn about things that the Indians contributed to Europe, from potatoes, medicines, and long-strand cotton, to hammocks and tobacco.

By the last decade of the 20th century, most historians saw Columbus as neither saint nor villain. Instead, historians placed Christopher Columbus somewhere in between. When writing his story they took note of all his qualities—bad and good.

This ship similar to the Santa María is from the illustrated edition
of Columbus's letter to the sovereigns published in 1493.

<hr>

—✦ NINE ✦—

YOU, THE HISTORIAN

Y NOW YOU HAVE COME A LONG WAY FROM SIMPLY looking up *Columbus, Christopher* in an encyclopedia. That was a good way to get an overview of his life. However, historians have found out much more about Columbus than you would read in an encyclopedia. That is why, at the end of the material about Columbus in an encyclopedia, you will find a bibliography. This is a list of books and documents from which the author of the encyclopedia entry got information. The list contains titles of secondary sources—books by other historians —and also any primary sources of information, such as original letters written by Columbus.

In nonfiction books too, you will often find bibliographies. These lists can help you do your research because they give you titles of other books to read. As you read these books, you will discover they also contain even more lists of books to read. (In this book, the bibliography is called "Sources of Information.")

Fairly soon in your research you may find that authors writing about the same subject often list many of the same books in their bibliographies. When so many authors found certain books especially helpful, you probably will too. For example, historian Samuel Eliot Morison wrote many books about Columbus between 1942 and 1974.

<hr>

Samuel Morison (third from right) with the crew of the Harvard Columbus Expedition

Most books about Columbus written after the 1940s list Samuel Morison's books in their bibliographies.

As you begin reading books about Columbus, you may notice that not all authors agree. You must decide which of them to believe. You have to ask yourself questions. Who seems the most reliable? Does the author have a prejudice that gives his or her book a bias?

As a historian, you will quickly learn a very important rule: Just because you see it in print does not make it true. Something can appear in several books, and still be wrong. A good example is the birth date of Columbus. One historian after another faithfully wrote it as 1435 because that was what the historian before had written.

If you follow the same trail others follow in their research, you will come to exactly the same conclusions and you won't have very much new to say. There is also a chance that it's the wrong trail. In doing research, what a historian hopes to find is some new bit of information that everyone else has somehow missed. If it is something about Columbus, then the historian can make an important addition to the Columbus story.

Besides using secondary sources of information, serious historians also try to find primary sources. Primary sources are the "raw material of history." In Columbus's case, the primary sources would be things that he wrote or that concerned him directly—such as his diaries, journals, and letters; the notes, or *postil*, in the margins of his books; government documents concerning him; and the notary records relating to him or his family. Other primary sources might be eyewitness accounts.

As a historian, you cannot always trust primary sources either. Here, too, you must ask yourself questions: Do I have enough evidence? Can I trust this witness? Is there some reason why a witness might be shading the truth or not telling the whole truth? Is this a hoax or a forgery?

A good example of when to be suspicious of primary sources is the case of the man who said he discovered a letter written by Columbus that washed ashore in a barrel—except that it was written in modern English, a language Columbus did not speak.

As a historian, the best way for you to be sure of your facts is to look for more than one clue. Like a detective, you need overwhelming evidence.

This was why historians were so pleased when some old notary documents turned up in Genoa in the 1800s. Now historians could prove that Columbus was Genoese. Besides his own statements that he was "of Genoa," and "from it [Genoa] I came and in it I was born," they had the official evidence from the notary records.

Several large libraries specialize in certain kinds of Columbus information to help historians in their research. A historian doing research on the *pleitos* could go to the Library of Congress in Washington, D.C. This huge library not only has a copy of every book published in the United States since the library began, but in 1941 the library's Manuscript Division acquired microfilms of the complete *pleitos*. And when the new *Raccolta* is published, many large libraries, such as the Library of Congress, will have copies.

The most famous collection of Columbus letters in the world is at the New York Public Library. The library's Rare Books Division

Trading with the Indians, as shown in the "Letter to Santangel." The illustrator did not understand the type of ships Columbus had: these are shown being powered by oars, not sail.

has printed copies of the original handwritten letter—now lost— that Columbus sent to the queen and king after his first famous voyage. There are copies in Spanish, Latin, German, and even Italian verse. But the most valuable of these is the first printed copy, dated 1493. It is called "Letter to Santangel" because Columbus addressed it to the treasurer of Spain, Luis de Santángel.

You won't be able to check out any of these rare documents, but the library has facsimiles, or copies, of the famous letters that researchers can see.

A modern view of the monastery of La Rábida. In addition to a gallery of Columbus portraits, it holds other materials about Columbus.

If you went to Europe, you could find libraries with even more valuable Columbus documents. At civic buildings in Genoa, Italy, you can see displays of the notary documents relating to his early life. In Spain, many libraries and museums contain Columbus documents and relics. There are facsimiles if the originals are too fragile to be on display. Seville has Biblioteca Colombina, an archive of some 3,000 volumes from the library of Columbus's son Ferdinand. Among the books are the ones with the marginal notes written by Columbus or his brother Bartholomew. Also in Seville is the Archives of the Indies, a collection of thousands of documents from the early days of the Spanish colonies.

At the Naval Museum in Madrid, there are primary source copies of Columbus documents, including those in the Martín Fernández de Navarrete collection. In Barcelona's naval museum, you will find not only boats, maps, and ships' models, but also a fine research library.

If you did some of your history research in Spain, you might even find a Columbus relic. You might find a paper with a clue to his strange signature in someone's attic, or you might even happen onto that "letter in a barrel" in an antique shop—although it is not very likely. Hundreds of historians before you have already done quite a thorough search.

There is always the chance, though, that you *might* find that missing document that Columbus scholars have been wishing for—perhaps even his original journal that has been lost for so long. And it would not necessarily have to be in Italy or Spain or Portugal. Since Columbus's time, invading armies have trooped back and forth across Europe, and soldiers have stolen many things. If they did take a Columbus relic or document, it could turn up anywhere in the world.

So if you were a historian sometime in the future and you did make a startling discovery, it could change some of the theories about Columbus that are held today. And it would be your turn to rewrite the history books once again!

SOURCES OF INFORMATION

The most helpful book I have found on how to do research is *The Modern Researcher* by Jacques Barzun and Henry Graff (Harcourt Brace Jovanovich, 1985). Also useful is *Research in Archives: The Use of Unpublished Primary Sources* by Philip Brooks (University of Chicago Press, 1969).

For information about Columbus and his time, some of the general history books I read were William Clark's *Explorers of the World* (The Natural History Press, 1964); *The World Awakes: The Renaissance in Western Europe* by Polly Brooks and Nancy Walworth (Lippincott, 1962); Genevieve Foster's *The World of Columbus and*

Sons (Charles Scribner's Sons, 1965); *Newsweek's Milestones of History,* volume 3: *Expanding World of Man* (edited by Neville Williams, 1970); *Discoverers of the New World* by Josef Berger (American Heritage, 1960); and Samuel Eliot Morison's *The European Discovery of America: The Southern Voyages* (Oxford University Press, 1974).

There are several interesting books about the discoverers of America who came before Columbus. These books include Patricia Lauber's *Who Discovered America?* (Random House, 1970); Stephen Krensky's *Who Really Discovered America?* (Hastings House, 1987); and G. R. Crone's *The Discovery of America* (Waybright and Tallen, 1969). Daniel Boorstin's *The Discoverers: A History of Man's Search to Know His World and Himself* (Vintage, 1985) is a remarkable book with much useful information about Columbus.

An excellent biography of Columbus for young people is Milton Meltzer's *Columbus and the World Around Him* (Franklin Watts, 1990). Jean Fritz's *Where Do You Think You're Going, Christopher Columbus?* (Putnam, 1980) is also a good biography, and fun to read. Among other Columbus biographies I read were Alice Dagliesh's *The Columbus Story* (Scribner's, 1955) and Gardner Soule's *Christopher Columbus: On the Great Sea of Darkness* (Franklin Watts, 1988).

The most well-known biography of Columbus is Samuel Eliot Morison's *Admiral of the Ocean Sea* (Little, Brown, 1942), which won a Pulitzer Prize. It contains a wealth of detail. I also read Gianni Granzotto's *Christopher Columbus: The Dream and the Obsession* (Doubleday, 1985), and Paolo Emilio Taviani's *Christopher Columbus: The Grand Design* (Orbis, 1985). Taviani, a native of Genoa, combed through his city's old records and official documents to establish Columbus's Genoese "roots." The biography *Columbus* (Macmillan, 1967) by the Swedish author and artist Björn Landström has handsome illustrations, including maps of Columbus's route and sketches of the way the author believes Columbus's flagship may have looked. (No one knows for sure.)

In *Sails of Hope: The Secret Mission of Christopher Columbus*

(Macmillan, 1973) Simon Wiesenthal suggests Columbus was Jewish and that his voyage was "a secret mission" to find a homeland for the Jews.

I found Washington Irving's *History of the Life & Voyages of Christopher Columbus* (my edition is Putnam, 1847) interesting because Irving was the first American biographer of Columbus and what he wrote in 1828 often differed from what later historians wrote.

Several books offer translations of the words of Columbus, his son Ferdinand, and his contemporaries. An important early 20th-century translator and editor of Columbus's writings was Cecil Jane, whose *Select Documents Illustrating the Four Voyages of Columbus* has been reprinted (Kraus, 1967). I also read Samuel Morison's *Journals and Other Documents on the Life and Voyages of Christopher*

Columbus (Heritage Press, 1963); *The Life of the Admiral Christopher Columbus by His Son Ferdinand*, edited by Benjamin Keen (Rutgers University Press, 1959); George Sanderlin's *Across the Ocean Sea: A Journal of Columbus's Voyage* (Harper & Row, 1966); and *The Quest of Columbus... from "the History and the Life and Actions of Admiral Christopher Colon" by Ferdinand Colon*, edited by Robert Meredith and E. Brooks Smith (Little, Brown, 1966). A more recent translation of Columbus's log of his first voyage is Robert A. Fuson's excellent book, *The Log of Christopher Columbus* (International Marine, 1987).

To get a feel for some of the trials and joys of present-day "hands-on" research, read Robert Marx's *Following Columbus: The Voyage of the Niña II* (World, 1964), which describes the author's voyage in a replica of Columbus's vessel. John Frye's *The Search for the Santa María* (Dodd Mead, 1973) tells of the problems of divers searching for Columbus artifacts in the Caribbean.

An important book and two articles examine the landfall question. *In the Wake of Columbus: Islands and Controversy* (Wayne State University Press, 1985), edited by Louis DeVorsey, Jr., and John Parker, summarizes the history of the controversy and offers many viewpoints. In his article, "Our Search for the True Columbus Landfall" in the *National Geographic* (November, 1986), Joseph Judge describes the National Geographic's expedition to try and find the landfall. "The Columbus Landfall" by Philip L. Richardson and Roger A. Goldsmith in *Oceanus* (Fall, 1987) suggests the final answer to the landfall question is still to be found.

❧ INDEX ❧

COLUMBUS EXPLAINING HIS DISCOVERY OF AMERICA TO KING FERDINAND AND QUEEN ISABELLA.—Drawn by ALEX GILBERT.—[See next page.]

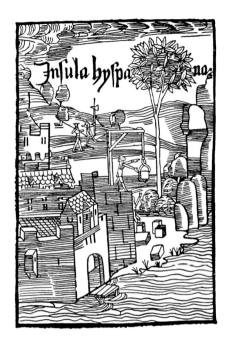

Illustration Acknowledgments: The maps on pages 12, 15, 20, 31, and 55 are by Laura Westlund. The other illustrations appear courtesy of Library of Congress, pp. 2-3, 16, 24, 32, 54, 59, 68 (2nd row, center), 76, 103, 109; Courtesy of Italian Government Travel Office, pp. 6, 10; New York State Library, p. 13; Knights of Columbus Headquarters Museum, pp. 17, 18, 48, 65 (left), 68 (2nd row, left and right; 3rd row, right), 69 (upper right, lower right), 86; Independent Picture Service, pp. 21, 28, 63, 68 (3rd row, left), 69 (center right), 71, 78, 91 (top), 94; James Ford Bell Library, University of Minnesota/Patricia Drentea, pp. 27 (left), 29, 30, 36, 37, 38, 46, 68 (top center), 81; The Mansell Collection, pp. 27 (right), 34, 56, 60, 62 (left), 68 (3rd row, center), 69 (lower left), 83, 89, 96, 100, 105, 111; Museo Naval, Madrid, pp. 41 (both), 44; Steve Johnson, pp. 43, 90 (top); Oregon Historical Society, p. 50; Organization of American States, p. 52; Columbus Memorial Library, OAS, p. 62 (right); The Greater Columbus Convention & Visitors Bureau, p. 65 (right); Ministry of Tourism, Bahamas, p. 66; Chicago Historical Society, p. 67; Chicago Public Library, Special Collections Division, p. 67 (inset); The Metropolitan Museum of Art, Gift of J. Pierpont Morgan, 1900, p. 69 (upper left); Bibliothèque Nationale, Paris, p. 72; Tourist Office of Spain, pp. 77 (top), 101; Massachusetts Historical Society, p. 77 (inset); Jamaica Tourist Board, p. 79; Courtesy of Woods Hole Oceanographic Institute, p. 85; Museum of the City of New York, p. 88; Museum of Modern Art of Latin America, pp. 90 (bottom), 92; Puerto Rico Federal Affairs Administration, p. 91 (bottom); Rare Books and Manuscripts Division, New York Public Library, Astor, Lenox and Tilden Foundations, p. 93; Harvard University Archives, p. 98. Cover design by Zachary Marell, front cover photograph by Bruce Christianson—back cover photo courtesy of Knights of Columbus Headquarters Museum.